Naturalistic Philosophies

OF

Experience

A Monograph in

MODERN CONCEPTS OF PHILOSOPHY

Series Editor

MARVIN FARBER

*State University of New York at Buffalo
Buffalo, New York*

Titles appearing in this series do not necessarily
reflect the thinking of the editor or publisher. The
series has been developed to present *all* modern
concepts of philosophy.
The following titles have either been published in
the series or are in production and will be
published soon.

Naturalistic Philosophies

OF

Experience

STUDIES IN JAMES, DEWEY AND FARBER
AGAINST THE BACKGROUND
OF HUSSERL'S PHENOMENOLOGY

By

D. C. MATHUR

*Professor of Philosophy
State University College of
New York at Brockport*

W A R R E N H. G R E E N , I N C .

St. Louis, Missouri, U.S.A.

Published by

WARREN H. GREEN, INC.
10 South Brentwood Blvd.
St. Louis, Missouri 63105

© 1971 by WARREN H. GREEN, INC.

Library of Congress Catalog Card Number 79-117613

Printed in the United States of America

TO MY PARENTS

PREFACE

IN this work, the author, through intensive and critical studies in the philosophies of James, Dewey and Farber against the background of Husserl's 'pure phenomenology,' has brought out at one stroke the limitations of the ultra-rationalistic brand of transcendental phenomenology with its ambitious 'constitutive' program, and at the same time opened a new and hitherto unexplored direction toward a naturalistic phenomenology of experience and knowledge. He has discovered not only in the writings of James (who has recently been studied extensively from the phenomenological point of view) but those of Dewey also, strong tendencies and incipient gropings toward such a consummation. He has brought out the inherent tensions in the attempts of James and Dewey to 'penetrate' nature through a descriptive-phenomenological analysis of experience. The author recalls how James constantly had to defend himself against the subjectivistic interpretations of his theory of 'pure experience' by critics, and how Dewey admitted the 'circularity' involved in his procedure in reply to his opponents. Nevertheless, James remains in the author's view a powerful precursor, and Dewey an able continuator, of an American brand of naturalistic phenomenology of experience and knowledge. And yet, these laudable attempts were hampered by that strange fascination for making an *absolute beginning* in philosophizing—which James and Dewey, despite their varied background and training, shared with Husserl. It is in the writings of Farber, who is heir to the tradition of both Husserlian phenomenology and American naturalism and realism, that the author finds a fully conscious and articulate development of naturalistic phenomenology based on a critique of the subjectivistic and idealistic implications of Husserl's later writings. Farber's principle of 'ontological monism' coupled with 'methodological pluralism' is seen to be free from the 'compulsive' search for a presuppositionless beginning. It places the phenomenological description of experience in its proper context of general methodology in which other methods, such as experimental inquiry, dialectical method of social-historical analysis, language analysis, and formal-conceptual analysis all play their legitimate role for a total understanding of man and his place in nature. Such a 'logically weighted' naturalism leaves out nothing which can be descriptively discovered and adequately supported by logical canons. In conclusion, the author emphasizes the importance of Farber's writings in performing the historical function of 'containing' the 'irrational' off-shoots of phenomenology in the various forms of 'existentialism,' retaining a cherished place for phenomenological analysis within general methodology, and working out a program of an adequately supported American brand of naturalistic phenomenology by drawing out the implications of a trend already discernible in the writings of James and Dewey.

ACKNOWLEDGMENTS

THE author gratefully acknowledges his indebtedness to *The Journal of Philosophy* for permission to make use of and reprint a major part of his previously published paper ("A Note on the Concept of 'Consummatory Experience' in Dewey's Aesthetics," vol. LXII, no. 9, April 28, 1966) in the eighth chapter of the present work. In the preparation and writing of Chapters V, VI, VII and VIII dealing with John Dewey, ample use has been made, with omissions and changes, of the author's unpublished Ph.D. thesis (The Significance of "Qualitative Thought" in Dewey's Philosophy of Art) submitted to Columbia University in 1955. Grateful acknowledgments are made to all concerned. The writer is especially thankful to the State University College of New York at Brockport for its assistance in getting the text typed for publication.

CONTENTS

CONTENTS

Naturalistic Philosophies

OF

Experience

Section A

WILLIAM JAMES

Chapter I

PHENOMENOLOGY OF EXPERIENCE

RECENT studies[1] in the philosophy of William James are shifting their emphasis from his pragmatism to his phenomenological insights. Attempts are being made to establish parallels between the thoughts and concerns of W. James and E. Husserl. While there are dangers of overdoing in this venture, there is a good deal of truth in the contention that there are strong phenomenological elements in James' philosophy. James was aware of the potentialities implicit in his descriptive and phenomenological 'flashes' as revealed in his *Magnum Opus, The Principles of Psychology,* 1890, and also in his *Essays in Radical Empiricism,* 1912. He overplayed his pragmatism against his 'radical empiricism' probably because the former aroused a much more heated controversy than the latter. He even went to the extent of saying in his preface to *Pragmatism* that, ". . . there is no logical connection between pragmatism, as I understand it, and a doctrine which I have recently set forth as 'radical empiricism.' The latter stands on its own feet. One may entirely reject it and still be a pragmatist."[2]

It will be our own endeavor to show that both his pragmatism and radical empiricism had a strong undercurrent of 'descriptive phenomenology,' which was first manifested in an impressive manner in *The Principles of Psychology*. It is well known that E. Husserl read the two volumes of this remarkable book, as well as his essay, "The Knowing of Things Together." He was impressed by James' descriptive psychology. The descriptive talents of James are in no way less than those of Husserl. The descriptive phenomenology of the early Husserl manifested in his *Logical Investigations, Phenomenology of Internal Time-Consciousness,* and the *Ideas* (section 27 to section 52, where he describes the natural attitude and its 'bracketing') makes superb reading. One can surely discover

5

some common attitudes in the thought of these two original and seminal thinkers.

Both James and Husserl made all of experience relevant to the philosophical enterprise, both of them made an attempt to undercut metaphysical disputes by making a 'return to experience' and both rejected a Humean conception of experience as totally inadequate. Though the present writer has no evidence that James ever read Husserl, it is interesting to find that in 'doing philosophy,' both were constantly concerned with *meanings*. And yet there are radical differences in outlook, temperament and training of these thinkers with consequent differences in the turn which philosophy took at their hands. Both claimed to be 'radical empiricists,' but in different senses. James wrote of "A World of Pure Experience" and Husserl was haunted by the ideal of 'pure' phenomenology, and spoke of pure experience. But this 'purity' had different significance and functioned differently in their respective philosophies. Husserl scholars differ in their interpretation of the development of his philosophy from the descriptive phenomenology of the *Logical Investigations* to 'transcendental idealism' envisaged in the Logos Essay, "Philosophy as Rigorous Science" and fully developed in *Ideen,* vol. I (1913) and *Cartesian Meditations* (1929).[3] Some scholars think that Husserl abandoned the early descriptive program and took a radical transcendental turn with *Ideen I.* Others maintain that the germs of transcendental subjectivity and idealism were implicit in the early phenomenological program and aims as adumbrated in the *Logical Investigations* and the Logos Essay. However, Husserl himself did not succeed in presenting his philosophy in a unified way. M. Farber best sums up the situation on this historical problem when he says:

"If one reads all of Husserl's writings consecutively, one cannot but be impressed by the *continuity* of his development. *But it would be absurd to disregard the great changes in Husserl's views* (thus, e.g., the 'phenomenological reduction' was not presented until 1913, in the *Ideas,* even though it was conceived and formulated some years earlier), or to discount his own repeated assertions concerning the important changes in his views"[4] (emphasis mine).

Husserl was a rationalist par excellence. His mathematical background and the influence of Descartes led him to the insatiable quest for 'absolute certainty' in knowledge. He dreamt of an absolutely presuppositionless 'First philosophy' which was also the vision of 'Final philosophy.' He conceived philosophy as a 'rigorous science' where rational 'seeing' or 'intuition' was to be final. This alone could, in his opinion, provide a firm, unshakeable foundation to all empirical sciences. This quest for absolutely certain knowledge required that he started from the 'foundations' and look for what is 'given' in experience. His excessive concern for 'purity,' 'certainty,' and 'self-givenness' led him to perform the famous *epoché,* and to 'bracket' the whole world of natural existence. This move from the natural attitude to the phenomenological attitude secured for him the requisite new realm of 'purified' being. It had its own grace, elegance and theoretical simplicity. It could provide a 'presuppositionless' starting point for all philosophical investigations. Nobody could disagree with such a phenomenological methodology provided one remembered that the natural world was only 'bracketed' but not 'nullified,' and that the new realm of 'essences' revealed thereby had no ontological implications for the status of consciousness. And Husserl himself was keen to avoid being interpreted as a subjective idealist when he said:

"We put out of action the general thesis which belongs to the essence of the natural standpoint, we place in brackets whatever it includes respecting the nature of Being: *this entire natural world therefore* which is continually 'there for us,' 'present to our hand,' and will ever remain there, is a 'fact-world' of which we continue to be conscious, even though it pleases us to put it in brackets."[5]

Yet this *epoché* and the consequent 'eidetic reduction,' though it opened a neat, elegant and pure realm of essences, made experience withdraw from the 'market place' to the 'cosy' atmosphere of a British drawing-room. There was only one step from 'bracketing' the world to 'nullifying' it. And this step was taken! One can find passages in Husserl which support both transcendental idealism (section 55 of the *Ideas*) as well as a self-sufficient absolute idealism, but not in the Hegelian sense. He wrote:

"Reality and world, here used, are just the titles for certain valid *unities of meaning,* namely, unities of 'meaning' related to certain organizations of pure absolute consciousness which dispense meaning and show forth its validity in certain *essentially* fixed, specific way."[6]

This passage from section 55 of the *Ideas* illustrates Husserl's transcendental idealism and assigns to consciousness the role of bestowing meaning. But there are other passages both in the *Ideas* and *Cartesian Meditations* that show that Husserl had to go beyond methodological phenomenology and take the 'transcendental turn' to subjectivity. He says:

". . . consciousness, considered in its 'purity,' must be reckoned as a *self-contained system of Being,* as a system of Absolute Being, into which nothing can penetrate, and from which nothing can escape; . . . which cannot experience causality from anything nor exert causality upon anything, it being presupposed that causality bears the normal sense of natural causality as a relation of dependence between realities."[7]

Again:

"Every imaginable sense, every imaginable being, whether the latter is called immanent or transcendent, falls within the domain of transcendental subjectivity, *as the subjectivity that constitutes sense and being.* The attempt to conceive the universe of true being as something lying outside the universe of possible consciousness, possible knowledge, possible evidence, the two being related to one another merely externally by a rigid law, is nonsensical"[8] (emphasis mine).

There is a conspicuous shift from regarding consciousness as an absolute existence in the *Ideas* to the Transcendental Ego with its constitutive acts in the *Cartesian Meditations*. One could legitimately apply the phenomenological method self-referentially and ask whether the Transcendental Ego is 'given' in phenomenological inspection, and whether the *occurrence* of the 'transcendental constitution' is open to phenomenological 'seeing.' Evidently 'pure phenomenology' breaks down here and Husserl slips from methodology to ontology without phenomenological justification. Consciousness or the Transcendental Ego has become a metaphysical 'absolute' and has, thus, overstepped its legitimate role of an epistemological 'absolute' for the bestowal of *meaning*. All this was made possible because Husserl cut off experience from its natural setting of 'hard reality.' Experience in its full-blooded nature is not 'pure,' 'rational,' 'necessary' and 'absolutely certain.' It shares the contingency of real life. An accident might put an end to consciousness. Moreover, the existence as well as the nature and structures of consciousness are dependent on the human brain and nervous system which are *contingent facts* of evolution and therefore could have been otherwise. M. Farber[9] rightly points out that Husserl commits the fallacy of 'illicit ignorance' in making consciousness a metaphysical absolute. Husserl's attempt to rationalize both the *form* and the *matter* of experience remains a dream—a grand vision incapable of realization. Speaking of Husserl's notion of experience (reduced to 'purity') M. Farber in his *Magnum Opus*[10] points out:

"Husserl has increased 'seeing,' or the field for description, offering a method for treating all types of experience. To attempt to use the phenomenological method *exclusively, with an artificial conception of experience,* as divorced from its natural status in the world and its cultural conditions, *would be to fail to do justice to experience itself in the complete sense of the term.* That would be to substitute metaphors for reality, and to miss the descriptive role of phenomenology" (emphasis mine).

Here, James differs most radically from Husserl. He did not have the monolithic methodological interest of Husserl, no quest for 'purity' (in Husserl's sense), 'absoluteness,' and 'certainty' of knowledge. He was a radical empiricist in a different sense. He enjoyed the contingency, 'raw feel' and the 'ruggedness' of the actual flow of 'lived' experience in its full-blooded warmth, concreteness and immediacy. He was temperamentally incapable of committing the fallacy of 'vicious intellectualism' by first abstracting natural essences from concrete experience and then setting them up, together with the intuiting consciousness, as metaphysical realities in their own right. He did not have the rationalistic visions of Husserl. In his most significant descriptive work, he kept close to the living flux of empirical experience in its *natural setting* and showed great phenomenological insight and superb skill in describing it. Though he made man's world, or the experienced world the main object of his life-long study, he never lost sight of the larger natural setting, the ever-receding horizon of novel and unexpected possibilities which enveloped the human scene. This natural world with its primeval quality of 'givenness' yielded only gradually to man's cooperative and cumulative efforts manifested in his 'cognitive' and 'conative' activities. In this way, a moralized and humanized world emerged out of his original world of unrealized potentialities, and James had a rare sensitivity and imaginative skill in describing this transformed and experienced world in all its color, variety and concrete occurrences, novelty and uniqueness. His pictorial and graphic descriptions were not meant simply for 'effect' but were meant to reveal the richness and to give us the 'feel' of the concrete details of the flow of experience. He first showed his extraordinary powers of observation and freshness of perception in the two volumes of *The Principles of Psychology* in the chapter entitled, "The Stream of Thought." His account of experience in this chapter was adumbrated by his earlier essay, "On Some Omissions of Introspective Psychology" (1884).[11] In his later essays, "Does Consciousness Exist?" (1904) and "A World of Pure Experience" (1904), together with "The Continuity of Experience" (1909), one can discern a shift to 'radical empiricism' and to the doctrine of 'pure experience.' In the first stage, James brought within experience the traditional dichotomy of self and not-self, of knower and known, of idea and object. These dichotomies were located in the ongoing flux of experience as reflective-cognitive distinctions which, in their turn, were embraced within an enriched and cumulatively growing experience. In this conception of 'radical' or 'pure' experience (the so-called second phase), James arrived at a 'neutral' view of experience which undercut the distinction between mind and body, the mental and the physical. He gave a different *meaning* to experience here and freed it from its exclusive association with consciousness as supposed by common sense. In other words, James was trying to give us the original 'feel' of *immediate experience* prior to all reflective distinctions and discriminations.

It will be interesting to note that though both Husserl and James[12] were appealing to immediate experience and to the finality of 'seeing' in philosophizing, yet their *conceptions* of 'immediate experience' were different. This observation supports the truth of M. Farber's contention that:

"Sooner or later, the choice between rival philosophies must lead to the inspection of experience. Only that does not necessarily mean much, *for everything depends upon the way in which experience is located and construed*"[13] (emphasis mine).

Husserl's radicalism and immediacy consisted in rationalizing both the matter and form of experience. This was achieved by 'bracketing' the natural world. The need for 'eidetic reduction' and 'transcendental reduction' was dictated by Husserl's insistent concern for 'purity,' 'certainty,' and 'absoluteness' of knowledge. What remained after 'eidetic reduction' was a realm of essences which were immediately 'given' in rational intuition. Experience was purged of its natural trappings and the stage was set for the final transcendental turn, and Husserl grappled with the most difficult task of 'transcendental constitution' in terms of transcendental subjectivity in the *Cartesian Meditations* and *Ideen II*. These essences were 'given' in intuition as well as 'constituted' by transcendental subjectivity. His concept of *primordial dator Intuition* (section 24, *Ideas*) conceives reason to be passive and receptive in intuiting essences. Speaking of the *Principle of all principles* he writes:

". . . *that very primordial dator Intuition is a source of authority (Rechtsquelle) for knowledge,* that *whatever presents itself in "intuition" in primordial form* (as it were in its bodily reality), *is simply to be accepted as it gives itself out to be, though only within the limits in which it then presents itself"* (*Ideas*, pg. 83).

That Husserl intended a 'spectator theory of knowledge' is evident in the following passage in section 23 of the *Ideas:*

"In particular, *essential insight is a primordial dator act,* and as such, *analogous to sensory perception,* and *not to imagination"* (pg. 83).

These passages, read with section 55 of the *Ideas*, give the impression that Husserl did, at one stage, take the 'given' as independent of consciousness and conceived the function of transcendental subjectivity as that of dispensing *meaning* only. This was in accord with Kantianism. But, as referred to above, there are passages both in the *Ideas* and *Cartesian Meditations* which point unmistakably to the grand program of Husserl to 'constitute' not only meaning, but the whole order of existence out of the depths of transcendental subjectivity. There is, therefore, a constant tension in Husserl's writings between the phenomenological program of describing essences and the transcendental one of 'constituting' not only 'meanings,' but reality also.

James, in contrast, emphasized the personal, changing, and continuous aspects of immediate experience, as is evident from his chapter on, "The Stream of Thought" in *The Principles of Psychology* (1890). His introspective and perceptive discoveries and discriminations were meant to bring out what was immediately 'felt' in the living flow of concrete experience. All the terms of discourse, such as, space and time, subject and object, qualities and relations, causal links, identity (sameness) and difference, together with a host of other syntactical connections, were referred back to original experience. The flux of immediate experience was composed not only of 'substantive parts,' the 'perches,' but also of the 'transitive parts,' the 'passages.' He had his own notion of evidence for any conceptual entity. To be 'real,' an entity had to be 'presented' in experience with its unique 'feel.' Even the 'subject,' or 'self,' which is usually opposed to the object and is supposed to be immune to this test had to present its credentials in the 'immediate feel' of experience. In this notion of immediate experience, James gave a place of prominence to the warmth and intimacy contributed by our organic sensations from the muscles, joints, lungs, etc. We shall return to this topic when we discuss his conception of self. James, like Brentano and Husserl, also emphasized the 'intentional' aspect of consciousness when he wrote:

"It always appears to deal with objects independent of itself" (*The Principles of Psychology,* pg. 225). However, this was not like the 'intentionality' meant by Husserl. The object here is not merely a 'meant' object, but the real, existing object in the world. What we experience directly and immediately is not any 'subjective' stream of consciousness, but historical objects of the real world. He agreed with John Dewey that, "experience is *of* as well as *in* nature. . . . Things interacting in certain ways *are* experience; they are what is experienced."[14]

James completely repudiates the Kantian distinction between the phenomenon and the *Ding-an-sich*. He wrote:

"Human thought appears to deal with objects independent of

itself; that is, it is cognitive, or possesses the function of knowing."[15]

Again:

"The judgment that *my* thought has the same object as *his* thought is what makes the psychologists call my thought cognitive of an outer reality."[16]

It was James' phenomenological insight into what is 'given' in immediate experience that saved him from the so-called insoluble problems faced by Hume and Kant. Both these latter philosophers had conceived experience to be a discrete and discontinuous series of sensations. It is because of this 'abstract' conception of experience that Hume found it impossible to give an intelligible account of the causal nexus and had to introduce the 'laws of association' *ab-extra* to account for continuities in experience, and Kant had to conjure up a trans-experiential source of unity in the form of the pompous 'Synthetic Unity of Apperception.' James, with his extraordinary gift in describing experience and rare analytical and discriminative skill in capturing the fleeting and the transient, the obscure and the subtle, found the connective tissue where it was present all of the time, i.e., in experience. He wrote:

"There is not a conjunction, or a preposition, and hardly an adverbial phrase, syntactic form, or inflection of voice, in human speech, that does not express some shading or other of relation which we at some moment *actually feel to exist* between larger objects of our own thought. If we speak objectively, it is the real relations that appear revealed; if we speak subjectively, it is the stream of consciousness that matches each of them by an inward coloring of its own."[17]

James thus evinced a unique capacity to articulate in reflective awareness the 'felt immediacy' of experience. And this reflective awareness, this conceptual 'knowledge about' had, in its turn, its own 'qualitative feel,' enriching the onward flow of experience.[18] Thus, not only the object is what it is 'experienced as,' but 'knowing about' is what is 'felt' to be.[18a] Perry, therefore, is sound in pointing out that, "His discoveries and descriptions were additive rather than reductive."[19]

James' view of experience entered its revolutionary stage with the publication of *Essays in Radical Empiricism*. The doctrine of radical empiricism and 'pure' experience was presented in his famous essays: "Does Consciousness Exist?," "A World of Pure Experience," "The Experience of Activity," and "The Continuity of Experience." Here he reduced the distinction of mind and body to a more primal stuff called 'pure' experience (interpreting it in a pluralistic manner) and gave a phenomenological account of the knower, the known and of knowledge. A detailed account of James' phenomenology of knowledge will be given in a later chapter. However, it may be noted that he arrived at the idea of pure experience and 'radical experience' after denying the existence of 'consciousness' as an *entity*. Here he was farthest away from Husserl, who adhered to the notion of consciousness and the transcendental Ego as subjective, and used the notions of 'radical' and 'pure' experience in the context of 'eidetically reduced' conscious experience. James spoke a different language when he wrote:

"To be radical, an empiricism must neither admit into its constructions any element that is not directly experienced, nor exclude from them any element that is directly experienced. For such a philosophy, *the relations that connect experiences must themselves be experienced relations, and any kind of relations experienced must be accounted as 'real' as anything else in the system.*"[20]

James, in keeping with the principle enunciated above, is seeking the "pragmatic equivalent" of consciousness in terms of 'realities of experience' after asserting that, "It is the name of a nonentity and has no right to a place among first principles."[21] By the terms 'pragmatic equivalent' and 'cash value' James meant the evidence of its presence in direct experience. He was attempting to give a phenomenological-descriptive account of consciousness and its 'function' in experience when he wrote:

"There is, I mean, no aboriginal stuff or quality of being, contrasted with that of which material objects are made, out of which our thoughts are made; but there is a function in experience which thoughts perform, and for the performance of which this quality of being is invoked. That function is *knowing*. 'Consciousness' is supposed necessarily to explain the fact that things not only are, but get reported, are known."[22] Advancing this thesis of 'pure experience' James writes:

"My thesis is that if we start with the supposition that there is only one primal stuff or material in the world, a stuff of which everything is composed, and if we call that stuff 'pure experience,' then knowing can easily be explained as a particular sort of relation towards one another into which portions of pure experience may enter. The relation itself is a part of pure experience; one of its 'terms' becomes the subject or bearer of knowledge, the knower, the other becomes the object known."[23]

Here James is giving experience a more comprehensive meaning than consciousness. 'Pure experience' or, the 'phenomenon' is not identical with conscious experience. In his concept of 'pure experience,' James is reducing both the physical and mental orders to the same primitive original components. Its 'purity' does not mean that it has been abstracted from its empirical context in the form of ideal essences as we would find in Husserl's eidetic reduction. It only means that pure experience is yet a 'potentiality' which in reflection can be articulated as 'mental' or 'physical' according to different functional and contextual roles. He repudiates the notion of consciousness as a metaphysical entity and seeks its meaning in 'pure experience' when he says that:

"Consciousness connotes a kind of external relation, and does not denote a special stuff or way, of being."[24]

In one of the most lucid passages, James describes pure experience as follows:

"The instant field of the present is at all times what I call the 'pure' experience. It is only virtually or potentially either object or subject as yet. For the time being, it is plain, unqualified actuality, or existence, a simple *that*. In this naif immediacy it is of course valid; it is there, we act upon it; and the doubling of it in retrospection into a state of mind and a reality intended thereby, is just one of the acts."[25] When asked to define the 'stuff' of this 'pure experience,' James says in his characteristic descriptive manner that,

"There are as many stuffs as there are 'natures' in the things experienced. If you ask what one bit of experience is made of, the answer is always the same: 'It is made up of *that*, of just what appears, of space, of intensity, of flatness, brownness, heaviness or what-not."[26]

True to a pluralistic phenomenology of experience, he continues:
"Experience is only a collective name for all these sensible natures, and save for time and space (and, if you like, for 'being')
there appears no universal element of which all things are made."[27]

James finds a corroboration of his view of 'pure experience' in
what are called our appreciative and value-experiences. He suggests that in the evolutionary process a lot of original, chaotic pure
experiences became gradually differentiated with an orderly inner
and outer world. In this process our 'appreciations' are neither
quite inner nor quite outer. He says:

"Experience of painful objects, for example, are usually also
painful experiences; perceptions of loveliness, of ugliness, tend to
pass muster as lovely or as ugly perceptions; intuitions of the morally lofty are lofty intuitions."[28]

Again:

"This would be the evolution of the psychical from the bosom
of the physical, in which the esthetic, moral, and otherwise emotional experiences would represent a half-way stage."[29]

In one of his most interesting and illuminating essays, "The
Place of Affectional Facts in a World of Pure Experience," included in his *Essays in Radical Empiricism,* James pursues further
his thesis of pure experience. The problem is to 'locate' our 'affections'–our pleasures, pains, loves, fears, angers, and the beauty,
comicality, preciousness, etc. of certain objects and situations. He
points out that these immediately 'felt' experiences are bathed in a
unique, pervasive quality which belongs neither to an 'outer' world,
nor an 'inner' world. The words 'outer' and 'inner,' he says, "are
names for two groups with which we sort experiences according to
the way in which they act upon their neighbor."[30] These are reflective distinctions within pure experience. Recommending Santayana's definition of beauty as 'pleasure objectified' he exhorts us
to note our language:

"The man is really hateful; the action really mean; the situation
really tragic–all in themselves, and quite apart from our opinion.
We even go so far to talk of a weary road, a giddy height, a jocund
morning or a sullen sky."[31]

Thus our affectional experiences remain equivocal and amphibi-
ous and do not belong exclusively to one realm or another. In our

interchange with things, objects come to acquire these 'affectional' or 'tertiary' qualities. James continues:

"It is these very attributes of things, their dangerousness, beauty, rareness, utility, etc.; that primarily appeal to our attention. In our commerce with nature, these attributes are what give *emphasis* to objects; and for an object to be emphatic, whatever spiritual fact it may mean means also that it produces immediate bodily effects on us, alterations of tone and tension, of heartbeat and breathing, of vascular and visceral action."[32]

James had conceived the principle of 'pure experience' as also a methodological principle which enunciates that "Everything real must be experienceable somewhere, and every kind of thing experienced must somewhere be real."[33] This is a sound phenomenological principle and James made use of it in describing 'pure experience.' However, James was not entirely consistent in his usage. The dominant tenor of his conception of experience is that of a 'neutral' stuff which in later reflection could be articulated as subjective or objective, mental or bodily, according to different functional and contextual relations. But sometimes he lapsed into a usage which suggests that experience and conscious experience were synonymous. This is because of strong commonsense 'mentalistic' association of 'experience.' In any case, the dominant conception of 'pure experience' is that of an 'original plenum,' the natural reality from which what commonly is called 'thought' makes selections, but all such selections, discriminations and abstractions transform and enrich the concrete flow of immediate experience. On the whole, such a world of 'pure experience' is orderly and predictable, but it still retains its "primeval dash of naughtiness" (in R. B. Perry's happy phrase) and manifests its immense complexity and measureless potentiality. And yet it is not an entirely chaotic, unstructured and discrete mass of sensations.

As has been mentioned earlier, R. B. Perry contends that James elevated his 'pure experience' to the status of metaphysical reality in his volume, *A Pluralistic Universe* in 'partnership' with Bergson. This is a controversial point, and can be argued both ways. An adequate treatment of this problem is possible only in the light of an analysis of James' view of 'reality' and 'rationality,' which will be attempted in a later chapter.

Chapter II

THE PROBLEM OF SELF

CONTEMPORARY philosophical literature is extremely 'self-conscious' about the problem of self. What exactly is the problem? What makes it a philosophical problem? And what method or methods are relevant for solving or 'disolving' such a problem? Descartes, the father of modern philosophy, brought it into sharp focus in his famous statement, *Cogito, ergo sum,* or "I think, therefore, I am." Descartes' radical separation of the 'I' as a thinking substance from the 'not-I' as a material substance had a freeing influence on both. The 'I,' or subject, was freed from mechanical determinism of matter, and the material substance was freed from 'mentalistic indeterminism' of the 'I.' At one stroke, it guaranteed moral freedom for the self, and a field for uninterrupted progress for the physical sciences. But it left a very tricky problem for philosophy as is evident from the attempts of Locke, Hume, Kant, Husserl, James, Dewey, Sartre, Merleau-Ponty, Wittgenstein and Gilbert Ryle, among others, to grapple with it.

The philosophical problem of the self centers on the questions: What is the *nature* of the self, or 'subject' or 'I'? And how do we *know* it? There are two major approaches, or philosophical methods which make a serious attempt to deal with it. It may at first sight appear that these two approaches are radically disparate. But a close look may reveal that they are not so far apart as they appear. I have in mind the phenomenological method and the method of ordinary language analysis made current by the 'later' Wittgenstein and his followers. The former method was brought into prominence, sharpened, and 'perfected' by E. Husserl and variously 'construed' by his followers. If we understand by phenomenological method a reflective analysis of the structures of experience as 'given' in their immediacy, and if following Wittgenstein we understand that language is a 'form of life,' or of lived

18

experience, then we can discover a close connection between these
seemingly different methods and approaches. While the method of
ordinary language analysis will raise the question of what the word
'I,' or 'self,' or 'subject' *means* in our language, the descriptive
phenomenologist will ask how the self or subject functions in immediate experience. Both of the enquiries are concerned with the
'meaning' of the 'self'—in immediate experience in the one and in a
language system in the other. The "systematic elusiveness" of the
"I" (à la Gilbert Ryle) and the similarity of the phenomenological
and the ordinary language approaches will be apparent if we consider how Husserl and Wittgenstein faced the problem.

In the *Tractacus* as well as *The Philosophical Investigations,*
Wittgenstein maintains a non-egological, 'no-subject' or 'no-owner-
ship' doctrine of consciousness. He distinguishes between various
uses of the 'I' and comes to the conclusion that in the expression
'I am in pain,' the 'I' does not refer to an *owner* of experiences, but
simply to the experience of feeling pain itself. The 'I' functions
here as a grammatical subject (like "it" in "it is raining") and not
as a transcendental, metaphysical subject or entity. He writes:

"The thinking, presenting subject—there is no such thing" (The
Tractacus 5.631-5.641).

Again:

"The subject does not belong to the world, but is a limit of the
world." (Op. cit.)

To me, it appears that this treatment of the problem resembles
the approach of Husserl in the *Logische Untersuchungen* where
descriptive phenomenology is prominent and as yet, no transcendental turn has been taken. The ego or the self is understood in
terms of the facts of consciousness. The ego means nothing apart
from the experienced unities of conscious acts or events. It is only
the organized totality of these acts. There is no place here for a
transcendental center apart and aloof from the experienced unities
of consciousness. This, as we shall see below in detail, bears a
great resemblance to the method used, independently of and earlier
than Husserl by W. James in his treatment of the consciousness of
self. Later on, as it is well known, in *Ideen I* and the *Cartesian
Meditations* Husserl, as a result of the various 'reductions,' arrived
at what are known as the 'three egos' and gave rise to the problem

of their identity. Commenting upon these three egos–(i) the world-immersed ego; (ii) the transcendental ego; and (iii) the epoché-performing 'observer,' M. Farber writes:

"What is at issue, in this distinction, is the *degree* of reflection; the transcendental ego, which ought to be taken in this sense, and not involve the cardinal principle of idealism, does not interfere with the 'world-belief,' thus allowing the world-immersed ego to remain valid. The transcendental, theoretical 'observer,' however, makes no use of any positing of the world, whether theoretical or atheoretical. Because it does not participate in the belief, the world is not valid for it simply, but only as a phenomenon, as the correlate of the transcendental belief which is thematized by this ego. It is indeed fortunate that this phenomenological trinity has not been exploited for theological purposes by those on the fringe of the movement."[1]

Thus, for the later Husserl, the 'pure ego' as contrasted with the empirical ego is not affected by the phenomenological reduction–which leaves us with the field of transcendentally purified experiences. If Husserl had remained true to purely descriptive phenomenology, he would have declared that such a pure or transcendental ego as identical and permanent is not to be discovered in the data of immediate experiences. It is the logic of his *method*[2] (with its 'reductions') that led him to posit the pure ego as "a nonconstituted transcendence–a transcendence in immanence" from which all acts of consciousness emerge. Therefore, besides the field of noeses and their noematic correlates there remains, over and above this, as a result of transcendental reduction, a 'pure ego' which is unaffected by the 'bracketing.' Though such an entity is situated within the domain of transcendentally purified consciousness, it transcends every specific act of this consciousness. Every intentional act of such a consciousness implies an object on the one hand and the same identical 'pure ego' on the other. It would be interesting to note that in America W. James grappled with this problem of the self in terms of descriptive phenomenology of experience in his *The Principles of Psychology* ("The Consciousness of Self") and *Essays in Radical Empiricism,* and made a heroic effort to avoid the positing of such a paradoxical entity–the 'pure ego' of Husserl which is neither noetic nor noematic. W. James kept close to immediate experience and searched for a meaning of 'self' in experience. His enquiry was a reflective analysis of our 'experience of the self'—of what is 'given' in the stream of experience. In a way, his method was both descriptive and analytical-descriptive because immediate experience was to be the locus for dealing with this problem, and analytical because he was constantly inquiring into the 'meaning' of 'self' in experience. If we accept Wittgenstein's thesis that language is a 'form of life,' we may say that W. James had great skill and ingenuity in analyzing 'meanings' in the context of the flux of immediate experience. He represents, in my opinion, a harmony of the two supposedly different methods referred to above—the descriptive-phenomenological and that of language analysis. It is the intention of the author to present in this chapter, W. James' analysis of 'self' in the context of his philosophy of radical empiricism. It may be emphasized that James' radical empiricism was firmly rooted in a realistic and naturalistic framework, as will be evident from his treatment of 'knowledge' and 'reality.'

James tells us that we speak of ourselves in the ordinary language as the sum total of what we can call *ours*. He says:

"In its widest possible sense, however, a man's Self is the sum total of all he *can* call his, not only his body and his psychic powers, but his clothes and his house, his wife and children, his ancestors and friends, his reputation and works, his lands and horses, and yacht and bank account. All these things give him the same emotions."[3]

He calls it the empirical self or 'Me' because it is the immediately *experienced* self and we identify ourselves with it in various degrees and experience self-feelings in connection with it. Here we have a phenomenology of the *experienced self* in terms of the *felt* emotions which our identification with it gives rise to. Truly speaking, the empirical self is not a bare unity but is composed of what James calls three constituents—the material self, the social self and the spiritual self. He gives acute and profound phenomenological analyses of these three selves. However, this is not all. If these are the *experienced* selves, who is the experiencer? James was thoroughly acquainted with the historical and philosophical problem of the 'I,' the 'Subject,' or the 'pure Ego' who is supposed to unify, or 'own' and be a 'witness' to the empirical flux of consciousness. He attempts to deal with the problem of the 'experiencer' in terms of a phenomenology of experience and sought to find a *meaning* of the 'I' or the 'Subject' within the flux of experience. He was clear in what he explicitly repudiated. He criticized the spiritualistic theory (soul-substance), the associationist theory (Hume and Mill) as well as the transcendentalist theory of Kant mercilessly. A careful reader of James' chapter on "The Consciousness of Self" will soon realize that these criticisms are advanced implicitly on the grounds of their being inadequate phenomenological descriptions of what is actually encountered in immediate experience. Summing up his arguments about the substantial soul, he says:

"My final conclusion, . . . is that it explains nothing and guarantees nothing. Its successive thoughts are the only *intelligible and verifiable* things about it, and definitely to ascertain the correlations of these with brain-processes is as much as psychology can empirically do"[4] (emphasis mine).

It should be remembered that James was not merely a phenomenologist of experience, but also a trained physiologist and scientist as well, and therefore, besides his phenomenological analyses we find him speaking of "correlations" of experiences with brain processes. James' criticisms of Kant's theory of transcendental Ego would apply roughly to even Husserl's doctrine of the pure Ego. He writes:

"The *ambiguity* referred to in the meaning of the transcendental Ego is as to whether Kant signified by it an *Agent,* and by the Experience it helps to constitute, an operation: or whether the experience is an event produced in an unassigned way, and the Ego a mere indwelling *element* therein contained. If an operation be meant, then Ego and Manifold must both be existent prior to that collection which results in the experience of one by the other. If a mere analysis is meant, there is no such prior existence, and the elements only *are,* in so far as they are in union. Now Kant's tone and language are everywhere the very words of one who is talking of operations and the agents by which they are performed. . . . Well, if it be so, Transcendentalism is only Substantialism grown shame-faced, and the Ego, only a 'cheap and nasty' edition of the soul. . . . The Soul truly explains nothing; the 'syntheses,' which she performed, were simply taken ready-made, and clapped on to her as expressions of her nature taken after the fact: but at least she had some semblance of nobility and outlook. The Ego is simply *nothing:* as ineffectual and windy an abortion as Philosophy can show."[5]

Further:

"The only service that transcendental egoism has done to psychology has been by its protests against Hume's 'bundle' theory of mind. But this theory has been ill-performed; for the Egoists themselves, let them say what they will, believe in the bundle, and in their own system merely *tie it up,* with their special transcendental string, invented for that use alone."[6]

In short, James rejects the transcendental Ego on the phenomenological ground that such an *entity* is not *presented* in the stream of experience and that a better account can be given of the 'unity' and continuity found in the flux of immediate experience. Before discussing James' analysis of the 'I' or 'pure Ego' it will be advisable to distinguish it from what he called the Spiritual Self–the third constituent of the empirical Me. James deals with the problem of personal unity in the context of the spiritual self as well as in connection with 'pure' Ego. By spiritual self he means, "a man's inner or subjective being, his psychic faculties or dispositions, taken concretely."[7] It is "either the entire stream of our personal consciousness, or the present 'segment' or 'section' of that stream, . . . both the stream and the section being concrete existences in time, and each being a unity after its own peculiar kind."[8]

James gives a very penetrating phenomenological description of the 'feel' of the central core of this spiritual self, and tries to come to terms with the problem of 'pure subjectivity' as such. He clearly mentions that in reflective awareness of the entire stream of spiritual self, we are thinking of ourselves as *thinkers.* For such 'subjectivity' all concrete psychical states–our pains, pleasures, thoughts, emotions, ideas, concepts, errors, illusions, etc. are objects. The 'thinker,' or 'subject' is therefore experienced *not* as an object but as an 'objectifier' in all its acts of identifications and dissociations. There is, therefore, an elusiveness about this innermost, central core of 'subjectivity.' To think or reflect directly upon *it* is to miss it because thereby we turn the 'subject' into an object. Speaking of this central core, he says:

"If the stream as a whole is identified with the Self far more than any outward thing, *a certain portion of the stream abstracted from the rest* is so identified in an altogether peculiar degree, and is felt by all men as a sort of innermost center within the circle, of sanctuary within the citadel, constituted by the subjective life as a whole. Compared with this element of the stream, the other parts, even of the subjective life, seem transient external possessions, of which each in turn can be disowned, while that which disowns them remains. Now, *what is this self of all other selves?*"[9]

James' description of the 'feel' of this *active* innermost self–the 'I' is superb. He says that some persons may think of it as a simple soul substance, or others may regard it as a pure fiction–an imaginary being denoted by the pronoun, I; but none disputes that this central nucleus of the self is *felt*. It would be rewarding to mention briefly his description of this felt experience of the pure subject. He was clearly conscious of the distinction between a 'felt experience' and our reflective awareness of it, between 'having' an experience and 'talking about' it in discourse. Speaking of it as an active, spiritual something which "seems to go out to meet" other contents of consciousness, he says:

"It is what welcomes or rejects. It presides over the perception of sensations, and by giving or withholding its assent it influences the movements they tend to arouse. It is the home of interest–not the pleasant or the painful, not even pleasure or pain, as such, but that within us to which pleasure and pain, the pleasant and the painful, speak. It is the source of effort and attention, and the place from which appear to emanate the fiats of the will."[10]

Further:

"It becomes opposed to them (other contents of consciousness) as the permanent is opposed the changing and inconstant."[11]

James gives another graphic and pictorial description of our experience of this *central spontaneity* in us when he says:

". . . I am aware of a constant play of furtherances and hindrances in my thinking, of checks and releases, tendencies which run with desire, and tendencies which run the other way. . . . The mutual inconsistencies and agreements, reinforcements and obstructions, which obtain amongst these objective matters reverberate backwards and produce what seem to be incessant reactions of my spontaneity upon them, welcoming or opposing, appropriating or disowning, striving with or against, saying yes or no. This palpitating inward life is, in me, that central nucleus which I just tried to describe in terms that all men might use."[12]

What is this innermost 'Subjectivity,' or the 'I' or the 'Thinker,' according to James? Is it a *substantial entity*—whether material or spiritual? We have seen that James rejects all attempts to identify the 'Subject' with a spiritual substance or with the transcendental Ego of Kant. In other words he remains a 'non-egologist,' in the sense that, without believing in a metaphysical Ego-entity, he gives a faithful descriptive account of the *felt* experience of such an innermost nucleus of the Self. James does not commit himself to any metaphysical explanation of this core of subjectivity. What he positively says about this 'feeling of subjectivity' might shock orthodox 'spiritualists' and Idealists of all brands. And yet James, with his background of physiology and with his skill as a phenomenologist, sticks his neck out when he says:

". . . coming to the closest possible quarters with the facts, *it is difficult for me to detect in the activity any purely spiritual element at all. Whenever my introspective glance succeeds in turning around quickly enough to catch one of these manifestations of spontaneity in the act, all it can ever feel distinctly is some bodily process, for the most part taking place within the head.*"[13]

Is James a gross materialist and epiphenomenalist? Is he an interactionist or a parallelist? Taking his later works such as *Essays in Radical Empiricism* and *Some Problems of Philosophy* into consideration it will be difficult to give a clear-cut answer to this question. He holds fast to a phenomenological description of experience with rare skill, ingenuity, insight and discriminatory capacity. He remains a thoroughgoing and radical empiricist and a functionalist in the sense that instead of indulging in metaphysical hypostatizations he inquires into the *function* of certain concepts such as the 'I,' the 'pure thinker' or 'unifying subjectivity' in experience. In *The Principles of Psychology* he comes to the following conclusion:

"That (in some persons at least) the part of the innermost Self which is most vividly felt turns out to consist for the most part of a collection of *cephalic movements* of *'adjustments'* which, for want of attention and reflection, usually fail to be perceived and classed as they are; that over and above these there is an obscurer feeling of something more; but whether it be of fainter physiological processes, or of nothing objective at all, but rather of *subjectivity* as such, of thought become 'its own object,' must at present remain an open question. . ."[14] (emphasis mine).

How then does James account for the sense of personal identity within the context of his descriptive analysis of the 'stream of thought'? What is the *meaning* of saying 'I am the same self as I was yesterday'? James, as a descriptive phenomenologist, says that in a sense there is no mystery involved in these judgments of *sameness*–whether they are made in the first person, second person or third. The intellectual operation involved in these judgments is that of subjective synthesis–of bringing things together into the object of a single judgment. This is essential in all thinking. "The subjective synthesis is involved in thought's mere existence. Even a really disconnected world could only be *known* to be such by having its parts temporarily united in the object of some pulse of consciousness."[15] But something more is involved in 'personal identity' than mere subjective synthesis of judgment. "It is the sense of a sameness perceived by thought and predicated of things thought about. These things are a present self and a self of yesterday. The thought not only thinks them both, but thinks that they are identical."[16]

James finds the clue to personal identity in the peculiar feeling of 'warmth and intimacy' with which our 'present self' is experienced. This is true of our 'bodily part' of it, also true of our more remote material, social and spiritual selves with which we are identified. We also feel the inner nucleus of the 'spiritual self' with great warmth either in the form of those faint *physiological adjustments* or of *pure activity of thought* taking place as such. He says:

"The character of 'warmth,' then, in the present self, reduces itself to either of *two* things, *something in the feeling which we have of the thought itself, as thinking,* or else the feeling of the body's actual existence at the moment, or finally–to both. . . . Any distant self which fulfills this condition will be thought with such warmth and intimacy."[17]

It is the *felt continuity* of our experiences and their *similarity* which gives them their peculiar warmth and intimacy. To this sense of 'animal warmth' our 'feel' of the 'same' body, despite changes of structure, contributes a lot. There is a great difference between another's body which I only see and my own which I see and *feel* at the same time. James, therefore, says:

"The sense of our own personal identity, then, is exactly like any of our other perceptions of sameness among phenomena. It is a conclusion grounded either on the resemblance in a fundamental respect, or on the continuity before the mind, of the phenomena concerned."[18]

As a realistic and empirical phenomenologist James attacks the problem of the pure Ego–the 'I' in connection with this sense of personal identity. He condemns any attempt to account for personal identity in terms of a "transcendent non-phenomenal sort of an Arch-Ego" and seeks its *meaning* in an *empirically and phenomenologically verifiable feature of our immediate experience.* He takes the problem out of a cloudy metaphysical haze and gives a full-blooded recognition to that 'warm' and 'intimate' feeling of our bodily existence which, according to him, "may be the absolute original of my consciousness of selfhood, the fundamental perception that *I am.*" It antedates Merleau-Ponty's attempt to account for it in terms of the 'lived body.' James' treatment may not satisfy those Idealists and Neo-Kantians whom nothing less than the pretentious and ponderous 'profundity' of the "Transcendental Ego or Observer" can bring relief. In analyzing our sense of 'personal identity' James is so faithful to immediate experience that he rules out the element of 'absolute unity' which the 'metaphysicians' are hunting for. No such 'absolute unity' is warranted by our 'experienced identity,' and it is going beyond 'evidence' to talk of it in such terms. James says:

"A uniform feeling of 'warmth,' of 'bodily existence' (or an equally uniform feeling of pure psychic energy?) pervades them all; and this is what gives them a *generic* unity and makes them the same in *kind*. But this generic unity coexists with generic differences just as real as the unity. . . . And similarly of the attribute of continuity; it gives its own kind of unity to the self–that of mere connectedness, or unbrokenness, a perfectly definite phenomenal thing–but it gives not a jot or a little more."[19]

Further:

"Resemblance among the parts of a continuum of feelings (especially bodily feelings) experienced along with things widely different in all other regards, *thus constitutes the real and verifiable 'personal identity' which we feel."*[20]

And yet, common sense and 'transcendental philosophers' are not satisfied because they are seeking for an 'absolute unity'–"a real belonging to a real Owner," and a pure spiritual *entity* of some kind. James is a sensitive and perceptive phenomenologist and comes very close to giving a phenomenological description of this sense of 'ownership' in the ongoing stream of our consciousness. This stream is continuous and cumulative and not a mere series of disconnected and disjointed elements. He assigns this act of 'ownership' or 'proprietorship' to the real passing, present onlooking, remembering, 'judging thought' or identifying 'section' of the stream. "This is what collects, 'owns' some of the past facts which it surveys, and disowns the rest, and so *makes a unity that is actualised and anchored and does not merely float in the blue air of possibility"*[21] (emphasis mine). For James then, "each Thought is thus born an owner, and dies owned, transmitting whatever is realized as its Self to its own later proprietor."[22]

This sense of 'ownership' is based on the experienced evidence of that 'warmth' which the passing Thought feels for its predecessors. That this phenomenological account is plausible enough is supported by cases of 'forgotten childhood memories' and split personalities where this 'warmth' is lacking and therefore the sense of 'personal identity' is lost. To those who insist that this 'act of ownership' or 'appropriation' is obscure because the 'passing Thought' cannot appropriate any other part of the stream of consciousness without *knowing 'Itself'* first–which, however remains unexplained in the above account–James says that there are two kinds of knowledge–one 'direct feeling of immediate existence,' and the other 'knowledge about' something. The passing Thought does not know itself in the sense of 'knowing about' but it does know itself in the sense of having a direct feeling of its existence. It would have been better if James had avoided the use of the word 'knowledge' for the 'immediate feeling of existence.' However, he is very clear about the distinction between 'having' an experience in immediate feeling and 'knowing about' it in later reflection. In an extremely clear passage he says:

". . . we must take care not to be duped by words. The words 'I' and 'me' signify nothing mysterious and unexampled—they are at bottom only names of *emphasis;* and Thought is always emphasizing something. Within a tract of space which it cognizes, it contrasts a *here* with a *there;* within a tract of time a *now* with a *then;* of a pair of things it calls one *this,* the other *that.* I and *thou,* I and *it,* are distinctions exactly on par with these, distinctions possible in an exclusively *objective* field of knowledge, the 'I' meaning for the Thought nothing but the bodily life which it momentarily feels."[23]

Thus the passing Thought is experienced in its immediate existence but nothing can be "known about" it until it is dead and gone. "Its appropriations are therefore less to *itself* than to the most intimately felt *part of its present object, the body, and the central adjustments,* which accompany the act of thinking, in the head. *These are the real nucleus of our personal identity,* and it is their actual existence, realized as a solid present fact, which makes us say, "as sure as *I exist,* those past facts were part of myself."[24]

James therefore concludes that the passing Thought is the thinker and so far as describing experienced facts is concerned no other non-phenomenal Thinker need be posited. Personality "implies the incessant presence of two elements, an objective person, known by a passing subjective Thought and recognised as continuing in time. *Hereafter let us use the words Me and I for the empirical person and the judging Thought"*[25] (emphasis in the original). "Thus the identity found by the 'I' in its *me* is only a loosely construed thing, an identity 'on the whole,' just like that which any outside observer might find in the same assemblage of facts."[26]

James confirms these conclusions in his later works. In his famous essay, "Does Consciousness Exist?" he denies the existence of consciousness as an *entity* and rejects the 'transcendental Ego' and calls it "only a name for the fact that the content of experience is *known. . . .*" "It is the name of a non-entity and has no right to a place among first principles."[27]

Searching for a descriptive-functional account of it, he says:

"There is, I mean, no aboriginal stuff or quality of being, contrasted with that of which material objects are made, out of which our thoughts are made; but there is a function in experience which thoughts perform, and for the performance of which this quality of being is invoked. That function is knowing."[28]

Again:

" 'Consciousness' is supposed necessarily to explain the fact that things not only are, but get reported, are known."[29]

Expounding his thesis of 'radical empiricism' or of 'pure experience' he finds a functional meaning of 'subjectivity' and 'objectivity' *within* the immediately felt flux of experience. He writes:

"Its subjectivity and objectivity are functional attributes solely, realized only when the experience is taken, i.e., talked of twice, considered along with its two differing contexts respectively, by a new retrospective experience, of which that whole past complication forms the fresh content."[30]

Again:

"The instant field of the present is at all times what I call the 'pure' experience. It is only virtually or potentially either object or subject as yet. For the time being, it is plain, unqualified actuality, or existence, a simple *that*. In this naif (sic) immediacy it is of course valid; it is there, we act upon it; and the doubling of it in retrospection into a state of mind and a reality intended thereby, is just one of the acts."[31]

James therefore reiterates in this Essay the basic findings of *The Principles of Psychology* in the chapter, "Consciousness of Self." The 'subject' as a 'transcendental' Ego or Observer vanishes together with the dualism of 'thoughts' and 'things,' and an account of the Kantian 'I think' is given on lines parallel with those found in *The Principles of Psychology*. He says in this essay:

"The 'I think' which Kant said must be able to accompany all my objects, is the 'I breathe' which actually does accompany them."[32]

In another famous essay, "A World of Pure Experience," James points out that his doctrine of radical empiricism locates all relations—conjunctive or disjunctive—within experience. The relations that connect experiences are themselves *experienced relations*. There is an immediate feel of even the most cognitive relations. As against Hume, J. S. Mill and Kant he holds that if 'conjunctive relations' are left out from the domain of experience, then the way is open for rationalists to admit to the existence of "trans-experiential agents of unification, substances, intellectual categories and powers, or Selves."[33] He points out all 'corruptions of dialectics' and 'metaphysical fictions' pour into philosophy if we do not keep close to direct experience of 'continuous change.' He exhorts us "to take it just as we feel it, and not to confuse ourselves with abstract talk *about* it."[34]

It is difficult to say how these views of James on the Self would fare if they were juxtaposed with his later interests and statements concerning religious and 'psychical' experiences. His range of interest was wide and he retained an open-mindedness with respect to all 'genuine' findings of experience. Some of his views in the essays, "Is Life Worth Living?" and "What Psychical Research Has Accomplished" are worth recording in this context. He says:

"I mean to use it (religion) in the supernaturalist sense, as declaring that the so-called order of nature, which constitutes this world's experience, is only one portion of the total universe, and that there are stretches beyond this visible world, an unseen world of which we now know nothing positive, but in relation to which the true significance of our present mundane life consists."[35]

Speaking about psychical experiences he says:

"The result is to make me feel that we all have potentially a 'subliminal' self, which may make at any time irruption into our ordinary lives. At its lowest, it is only the depository of our forgotten memories; at its highest, we do not know what it is at all."[36]

It is an open question whether these statements are incompatible with his earlier analysis of the Self or they add a new dimension to his radical empiricism—the full implications of which have yet to be drawn.

Chapter III

MIND, KNOWLEDGE AND TRUTH

PHILOSOPHICAL disputes about the nature, certainty and objectivity of knowledge have a long historical past. While the natural sciences were accumulating useful knowledge in various fields with the help of a self-correctible scientific methodology, philosophers continued to wrangle over the nature of knowledge and even questioned the very possibility of it. One need only be reminded of the centuries-old dispute between empiricism and rationalism to realize how long and weary the battle has been. The specific issues concerning the so-called problem or problems of knowledge are therefore historical in nature. They are predominantly 'problems of philosophers' rather than 'problems of men' (à la Dewey). One need not be surprised if one discovered a deep-seated social motive underlying the interminable dispute between rationalism and empiricism.[1] And yet it will be an error to suppose that any such neat social-historical motive could exhaust and explain away the entire problem of knowledge. The way or ways in which the problem has been posed may reveal also what M. Farber[2] has called a 'methodogenic' bias as well as unexamined standpoint commitments. And lastly some of the problems at least could be genuinely 'empiriogenic' arising within the ongoing stream of experience itself. It is therefore important to disentangle the various tangled strands of the so-called problem of knowledge. W. James inherited the problem of knowledge as a historical legacy. It was couched in the dualistic framework handed down by Descartes and confirmed by the 'ponderous' Kant. The immediate philosophical stimulus was provided by the Absolute Idealism and Transcendentalism of post-Kantian thinkers such as Bradley and Royce. The reigning tendency of the times challenged the ingenuity of James in solving the problem of knowledge and he responded to it in an extremely original and fresh manner. In brief, the problem which

James faced was: How could an *idea* know its *object?* How could the *knower* know the *known?* The assumptive commitment here was to an extreme dualism of mind and matter, Subject and Object, the Knower and the Known. If idea (belief, opinion, etc.) was something mental and subjective, and the object was material and external to it, how could the one know the other? How could a knower, a mind, know the object? How could the gulf be bridged? If knowledge was to be possible the idea had to somehow 'leap' across the hiatus to meet the object. Thus, the problem of the 'transcendence' of the object in the cognitive situation called for serious attention. It will be interesting to note here that James was adopting the same descriptive-phenomenological method for inquiring into the concrete knowledge-situation which E. Husserl was applying to the solution of a similar problem in his *Logical Investigations* (studies 5 and 6). Both bypassed the Kantian formulation of the problem as: How is knowledge possible? and proceeded to inquire into the nature of the object as well as the nature of knowledge and the ways of knowing. It was clearly a *phenomenology of knowledge* which both were attempting in tackling this problem. Thus, in an early essay, "The Function of Cognition" published in *Mind,* vol. X (1885) James wrote:

"The following inquiry is . . . not an inquiry into the 'how it comes,' but into the 'what it is' of cognition. . . . In it we shall simply assume that cognition *is* produced, somehow, and limit ourselves to asking what elements it contains, what factors it implies."[3] Further:

"In short, our inquiry is a chapter in *descriptive psychology*– hardly anything more"[4] (emphasis mine).

James wrongly called his procedure here 'descriptive psychology.' He ought to have called it descriptive phenomenology because, in its actual practice James was carrying out a reflective analysis of the cognitive situation–of its essential structure. This is what Husserl was doing in his *Logical Investigations.* And yet by a historical coincidence Husserl also labeled his phenomenology as descriptive psychology in the *Logical Investigations* (2:4, vol. I ed., 1901). However, Husserl corrected himself in the second edition of the *Logical Investigations* and dropped the phrase 'descriptive psychology' in favor of 'descriptive phenomenology.' He conceived pure phenomenology as a "sphere of neutral investigation in which various sciences have their roots" and gave acute analyses of idea, knowledge, judgment, and traced the fundamental concepts to their 'sources' (not in a generic manner) in immediate reflective experience–to epistemological clearness and distinctness. It was not merely a symbolic understanding of words but was a "going back to things themselves" in order to fix all meanings in their concrete fullness and 'self-givenness' in original 'categorial intuition.' This task of phenomenological 'clarification' of fundamental logical concepts occupied Husserl completely at this stage, and philosophical literature has been enriched by his insightful analyses of the concepts of 'expression,' meaning, idea, object, etc. His analysis of the cognitive situation in terms of the distinctions of the physical sign or complex, the intentional acts (meaning-giving and meaning-filling), the meanings (as ideal unities) and the object intended, is now well-known. All this was admirable, and Husserl had not yet taken the 'transcendental turn.' To me it appears that his mathematical background made him conceive the philosophical task as even more 'rigorous' than mathematics itself, since mathematical concepts themselves were to be traced to their 'sources' in their phenomenological 'givenness' in concrete intuition. This search for 'absoluteness' in knowledge, this quest for 'foundations,' this rationalistic vision, gave Husserl's writings an awe-inspiring rigour which has not since been equalled. But it is also responsible for his 'discovering' this certainty and absoluteness in Subjectivity and the Transcendental Ego (the *Ideas* and the *Cartesian Meditations* bear testimony to this). The methodological preoccupation with absoluteness not only necessitated a return to Subjectivity but gave rise to the most difficult problem of 'constituting' the other egos and the 'world'–with which Husserl grappled heroically but without much success. This excessive concern with methodological rigour proved a trap, and Husserl got entangled in the 'idealistic' and 'subjectivistic' notions of Consciousness and the Ego.

James, while adopting the same method of descriptive analysis of cognitive experiences, questioned the very meaning of 'consciousness' and 'subjectivity' in terms of what he conceived to be 'pure experience.' He did not feel the need for 'bracketing' the 'world' or other 'egos.' He had a knack for keeping close to the changing and the contingent flow of experience and gave a descriptive account of both perceptual and conceptual knowledge without surrendering the naturalistic and realistic context in which human experience finds itself. In short, James' philosophy may be regarded as oriented towards a 'naturalistic phenomenology' as contrasted with the Transcendental Phenomenology of Husserl, though at times he departed from it. It will be our endeavor to show how James' treatment of the problem of knowledge is basically a descriptive-phenomenological analysis without 'idealistic' entanglements of any kind.

James' analysis of the cognitive situation bears the imprint of his training in physiology, medicine and evolutionary biology. The 'temporal factor' enters into his reflective analysis in a manner which it never does in Husserl's analysis with its mathematical background. In other words James calls his theory 'ambulatory' in terms of a chain of experiences whereas Husserl's analysis is entirely 'cross-sectional.' In any knowledge-situation we have on the one hand an idea, mind or consciousness and on the other hand an object. But what is this 'mind' or 'consciousness'? Who is this knower? James does not conceive this knower in terms of disembodied consciousness. For him the knower is the man, the organism in interaction with a changing natural and social environment. Mind or Consciousness as an *entity* does not exist for him as we have seen in the last chapter. He conceived a descriptive phenomenology of 'mind' as a prerequisite for the understanding of the cognitive situation. He gives a descriptive analysis of mind or consciousness in various works including *The Principles of Psychology,* "Does Consciousness Exist?" *(Essays in Radical Empiricism)* and "The Experience of Activity" *(Essays in Radical Empiricism)* and in his *A Pluralistic Universe.* He points out that we know 'mind' not as a substantial entity, but by what it *does,* its operations and activities. The organism with its selective interests is in dynamic interaction with the environment. It shows care, concern, develops foresight, makes effort and suffers frustration or feels satisfaction; it 'knows,' 'believes,' etc., etc. All these activities describe and constitute 'mind' in concrete, experiential terms. Mind is a selective agency. It responds, with its selective interests, to the differentiated flow of 'pure experience' and carves out a 'human' world. The sense organs and the 'attentive,' 'thinking' and 'reasoning' capacities perform the function of selecting relevant portions of 'primitive experience.' Mind is thus a 'theater of simultaneous possibilities.'⁵ We saw in the last chapter how he gave a functional and relational view of consciousness and dismissed any 'transempirical unifier' in the form of an alleged transcendental ego as simple moonshine. He gave an extremely acute phenomenological analysis of our 'individualized self' or 'mind' in his famous essay "The Experience of Activity,"⁶ which was essentially a continuation of his equally able analysis of Self in *The Principles of Psychology*. He traced the meaning of 'activity' not merely in a linguistic context, but to its source in the stream of experience and unravelled its function in the flux of experience. It was in this essay that he propounded his famous 'methodological postulate' which he termed as 'pragmatic method' or the 'principle of pure experience' but which may rightly be called the phenomenological method of analysis of concepts in terms of immediate experience. He wrote:

"The pragmatic method starts from the postulate that there is no difference of truth that doesn't make a difference of fact somewhere; *and seeks to determine the meaning of all difference of opinion by making the discussion hinge as soon as possible upon some practical or particular issue. The principle of pure experience is also a methodological postulate. Nothing shall be admitted as fact, it says, except what can be experienced at some definite time by some experient;* and for every feature of fact ever so experienced, a definite place must be found somewhere in the final system of reality. In other words: *Everything real must be experience-able somewhere, and every kind of thing experienced must somewhere be real*"⁷ (emphasis mine). James regarded our 'experience of activity' as constituting the very core of our 'individualized self' or mind. He wrote:

". . . in the actual world of ours, as it is given, a part at least of the activity comes with definite direction; *it comes with desire and sense of goal, it comes complicated with resistances which it overcomes or succumbs to, and with the efforts which the feeling of resistance so often provokes;* and it is in complex experiences like these that the notions of distinct agents, and of passivity as opposed to activity arise. Here also the notion of causal efficacy comes to birth."[8]

He continues:

"If the word has any *meaning*, it must denote what there is found. *There* is complete activity in its original and first intention. *What it is 'known as' is what there appears.* The experience of such a situation possesses all that the idea contains. *He feels the tendency, the obstacle, the will, the strain, the triumph, or the passive giving up,* just as he feels the time, the space, the swiftness or intensity, the movement, the weight and color, the pain and pleasure, the complexity or whatever remaining characters the situation may involve."[9]

Further:

"The *percipi* in these originals of experience is the esse; the curtain is the picture. If there is anything hiding in the background, it ought not to be called activity, but should get itself another name."[10]

In his reply to Stout's criticism of his position in *The Principles of Psychology*, Vol. I where James identified *spiritual* or *mental activity* with certain muscular feelings and intracephalic movements (see his chapter on "The Consciousness of Self"), James points out that Stout does not keep the distinction between 'our' activity and the 'total experience-process' clear. James reaffirms and clarifies his position and incidentally gives a graphic descriptive analysis of 'our self' or "our mind or consciousness" in naturalistic terms. There is no consciousness as such, no mind as such, and no activity as such. In one of his most famous and distinctive passages, he points out:

"*The individualized self*, which I believe to be the only thing properly called self, *is a part of the content of the world experienced*. The world experienced (otherwise called the *'field of consciousness'*) comes at all times with *our body as its center*, center of vision, center of action, center of interest. Where the body is is 'here'; when the body acts is 'now'; what the body touches is 'this'; all other things are 'there' and 'then' and 'that' . . . *The body is the storm center, the origin of coordinates, the constant place of stress in all that experience-train.* Everything circles round it, and is felt from its point of view. *The word 'I,' then is primarily a noun of position, just like 'this' and 'here.'* Activities attached to 'this' position have prerogative emphasis, and, if activities have feelings, must be felt in a peculiar way. The word 'my' designates the kind of emphasis. I see no inconsistency whatever in defending, on the one hand, 'my' activities as unique and opposed to those of outer nature, and, on the other hand, in affirming, after introspection, that they consist in movements in the head. The 'my' of them is the emphasis, the feeling of perspective interest in which they are dyed."[11]

Here James is giving us a naturalistic phenomenology of 'mind.' The elements of the natural environment selected by the dynamically interested organism (the body remains the original instrument of selection and center of interest) constitute the contents of the 'mind.' These contents have their own characteristics, traits and patterns which were not found in the 'untransformed' elements of nature. James, in descriptively accounting for the mind and its properties, thus, does not fall in the 'deep sea' of 'mechanical reductionism' in order to escape the 'devil' of 'subjectivism.' One of the most significant characteristics of this 'group of contents' called the mind, is the knowing-process. We, therefore, pass on to James' analysis of this cognitive process.

James' method of tracing concepts to their source in 'immediate experience' is phenomenological and is entirely different from the 'psychologistic' positivism of Locke, Berkeley, Hume and J. S. Mill. In trying to account for the phenomenon of knowledge or cognitive experience in terms of its evidence in immediate experience he was trying to oppose 'dualism' as well as 'transcendentalism.' It was a more thoroughgoing descriptive analysis than had been attempted by the so-called positivists mentioned above. That it was a search for clarity is shown by an unpublished letter which he wrote in 1888 to the psychologist Ribot:

"Empirical facts without 'metaphysics' will always make a confusion and a muddle. I'm sorry to hear you still disparage metaphysics so much, since rightly understood, the word means only the search for *clearness* where common people do not even suspect that there is any lack of it. The ordinary positivist has simply a bad and muddled metaphysics which he refuses to criticize or discuss."[12]

Though by his reflective analysis of cognitive experience, James came to the conclusion that things are "what they are known as," he never held the idealistic doctrine that, therefore, knowing 'constitutes' their being. Things need not be known in order to be. In order to show this he gave a detailed description of the knowing process in his *Essays in Radical Empiricism* and *A Pluralistic Universe*, to supplement and elaborate what he had said in his *Pragmatism* and *The Meaning of Truth*. He shared with J. Dewey a functional or instrumental theory of knowledge but the method which he adopted was that of descriptive analysis. For him then, there are two kinds of knowledge: direct, immediate perceptual knowledge called 'knowledge by acquaintance,' and indirect, representative or substitutional knowledge called, 'knowledge about.' He points out that all attempts to understand the cognitive relation in both these cases have been bogged down in an almost insoluble and artificial problem of the relation between the 'knower' and the 'known,' the 'subject' and the 'object.' Once these two have been assumed to be *discontinuous entities,* the artificially produced 'chasm' between them could never be bridged. All the so-called representative theories (Locke), commonsense theories and transcendental theories commit this error, and are not *radical* enough to trace this relation to its very source in immediate experience. In other words, there is no *adequate* analysis of these concepts of the knower and subject on the one side and the known and object on the other side. He therefore says: "Either the Knower and the Known are:

"(1) The self-same piece of experience taken twice over in different contexts; or they are

"(2) Two pieces of *actual* experience belonging to the same subject, with definite tracts of conjunctive transitional experience between them; or

"(3) The known is a *possible* experience either of that subject or another, to which the said conjunctive transitions would lead, if sufficiently prolonged."[13]

The first type of knowledge is direct, perceptual knowledge and the other two are indirect knowledge where the mind (to be understood in the way described earlier) has 'knowledge about'[14] an object not directly given. Let us first understand his account of perceptual direct knowledge. What occurs in the perceptual situation? In direct perceptual knowledge "any one and the same *that* in experience must figure alternately as a thing known and as a knowledge of the thing, by reason of two divergent kinds of context into which, in the general course of experience, it gets woven."[15]

It means that the *same* piece of 'pure experience' in one *context* is a thing of 'outer nature,' and in another context (i.e. the context of consciousness or direct knowing by the interested organism) it is knowledge or conscious content. The thing *itself* is acted on by the mind (understood in James' sense) and *felt* as an item of conscious experience. Here then, in 'presentative' knowledge the 'idea' or 'percept' is a fragment of the 'object' or 'thing' itself. It does not 'copy' it in a mysterious way. In other words, the object is given as it is in direct experience through its various appearances. James says:

"*Experience* . . . has no inner duplicity; and the separation of it into consciousness and content comes, not by way of subtraction but by way of addition—the addition to a given concrete piece of it, of other sets of experiences, in connection with which severally its use or function may be of two different kinds."[16]

Again:

"Just so, I maintain, does a given undivided portion of experience, taken in one context of associates, play the part of a knower, of a state of mind, of consciousness; while in a different context, the same undivided bit of experience plays the part of a thing known, of an objective content."[17]

Giving an illustration of our perceptual experience of a room, James says:

"In one of these contexts it is your 'field of consciousness'; in another it is the 'room in which you sit'; *and it enters both contexts in its wholeness, giving no pretext for being said to attach itself to consciousness by one of its parts or aspects, and to outer reality by another*"[18] (emphasis mine).

Here we find that James' theory of "pure experience" as something neutral, and his account of the two contexts or functional relations into which the same piece of "pure experience" may enter in its wholeness as a thing known and the knowing of it, helped

him in giving a non-dualistic description of the perceptual situation. But is it true that an object or a thing as a *whole* gets into a
conscious relationship at one time in perception? Husserl's analysis
of the perceptual situation in terms of the intentional act, the vary-
ing perspectival appearances of an object, and the ideal identity of
the intended object, seems to do more justice to the complexity of
the facts. And yet, Husserl adhered to a 'subjectivistic' or 'idealistic' view of consciousness whereas James on the whole avoided this
'subjectivism' by an analysis of consciousness and experience in a
functional way. James thus operated within a predominantly naturalistic and realistic framework,[19] while Husserl became enmeshed
in methodological puzzles of the idealistic position. In his treatment
of 'concepts' James, like the later Husserl, avoided 'psychologism'
and spoke of his doctrine as 'logical realism' (different from Pla-
tonism). He, again like Husserl, distinguished between the experience of logical or mathematical entities and their 'objectivity' and
'reality' as ideal entities. Speaking of concepts, memories or fancies
as bits of pure experience he regarded them as *thats* which "act in
one context as objects, and in another context, figure as mental
states."[20]

Again:

". . . and that one forms the inner history of a person while the
other acts as an impersonal objective world, either spatial and
temporal, or else merely logical or mathematical, or otherwise
'ideal.' "[21]

Since James did not bring out clearly the relation between the
occurrence or *experience* of 'ideal' entities in the personal history
of an individual and their logical status as 'objective' in some sense
as a coordinate realm of reality, he was obliged to say that his
philosophy:

"may be regarded as somewhat eccentric in its attempt to com-
bine logical realism with an otherwise empiricistic mode of
thought."[22] It may however be added that James was aware of the
rise of the new literature on logic and mathematics in his time.[23]

James' analysis of conceptual knowledge may be gathered from
several essays. In "The Function of Cognition"[24] and "The Tigers
in India"[25] James analyzed the relation between an *idea* (also called

opinion, belief or statement) and *object* in terms of two factors, *intention and agreement* (or fulfillment). He continued the descriptive analysis in his famous essay "A World of Pure Experience."[26] When we say we have an idea of the "tigers in India" we *mean, intend,* or *refer* to them. This intending is prior to agreement and is an active and practical affair. It is like a plan of action *directed* to the object intended which is our goal or terminus. He wrote:

"The pointing of our thought to the tigers is known simply and solely as a procession of mental associates and motor consequences that follow on the thought, and that would lead harmoniously, if followed out, into some ideal or real context, or even into the immediate presence, of the tigers. . . . In all this there is no self-transcendency in our mental images *taken by themselves.* They are one phenomenal fact; the tigers are another; and their pointing to the tigers is a perfectly commonplace intra-experiential relation, *if you once grant a connecting world to be there.*"[27]

The so-called *agreement* of an idea with its object was first conceived by James to be that of resemblance.[28] But he soon realized that *agreement* too was to be understood *not* in the passive sense of 'copying' of an object by the idea, but in terms of a practical connection. An idea agrees with its intended object if it *fits* it (as a key fits its lock or 'words' fit objects) in the sense of leading up to it and putting us in direct perceptual contact with it. He says:

". . . if I can lead you to the hall, and tell you of its history and present uses; if in its presence I feel my idea, however imperfect it may have been, to have led hither and to be now terminated," then, "that percept was what I *meant,* for into it my idea has passed by conjunctive experiences of sameness and fulfilled intention."[29] Again he gives a descriptive analysis of the cognitive experience when he says:

"Whenever certain intermediaries are given, such that, as they develop towards their terminus, there is experience from point to point of one direction followed, and finally of one process fulfilled, the result is that *their starting point thereby becomes a knower and their terminus an object meant or known.* That is all that knowing (in the simple sense considered) can be known-as, that is the whole of its nature, put into experiential terms."[30]

James calls the experience that knows another as its *substitute* or *representative* in the sense that "by experimenting on our own ideas of reality, we may save ourselves the trouble of experimenting on the real experiences which they severally mean."[31] Denying that there is any mystique of the union of the Knower and the Known in Knowledge James says:

"But union by continuous transitions are the only ones we know of, whether in this matter of a knowledge-about that terminates in an acquaintance, whether in personal identity, in logical predication through the copula 'is,' or elsewhere. . . . These are what the unions are *worth*, these are all that *we can ever practically mean by union, by continuity.*"[32]

He sums up his position on the nature of knowledge in the context of his view of 'pure experience' when he says,

"The instant field of the present is always experience in its 'pure' state, plain unqualified actuality, a simple *that*, as yet undifferentiated into thing and thought, and only virtually classifiable as objective fact or as someone's opinion about fact. This is as true when the field is conceptual as when it is perceptual."[33]

James brought his naturalistic phenomenology, in the context of his view of 'pure experience,' to bear on the problem of 'other minds' and that of 'sharing' a common world. This problem has gripped the contemporary philosophical world following its discussion by Husserl in his treatment of the transition to intersubjectivity from the experiences of an individual experiencing Ego. Husserl, having entered into Transcendental Subjectivity, found it an extremely difficult and tricky problem to account, by way of 'constitution,' for the other egos and a common objective world. The Fifth Meditation of his *Cartesian Meditations* makes difficult reading on this issue. James rejected the 'idealistic' view of mind or consciousness, and branded the notion that our objects are 'inside' our respective 'minds' or 'heads' as absurd. Repudiating the radical separation of 'body' and 'mind' he gave a descriptive account of how one becomes aware of another 'mind.' He wrote:

"In that perceptual part of *my* universe which I call *your* body, your mind and my mind meet and may be called coterminus. Your mind actuates that body and mine sees it; my thoughts pass into it as into their harmonious cognitive fulfillment; your emotions and volitions pass into it as causes into their effects."[34]

Again:

"Practically, then, our minds meet in a world of objects which they share in common, which would still be there, if one or several of the minds were destroyed."[35]

And he gives, in the light of his descriptive analysis of mind, an account of how the same objects can be 'shared' by a number of minds. He writes:

". . . a mind or personal consciousness is the name for a series of experiences run together by certain definite transitions, and an objective reality is a series of similar experiences knit together by different transitions. If one and the same experience can figure twice, once in a mental and once in a physical context, one does not see why it might not figure thrice, or four times, or any number of times, by running into as many different mental contexts, just as the same point lying at their intersection, can be continued into different lines."[36]

James' concept of 'agreement' of an idea with its intended object brings us to his theory of *truth*. The historical controversy over the so-called pragmatic theory of truth propounded by James and supported by Schiller and J. Dewey (though with different emphases) is now well known. There is no doubt that the theory has been grossly misunderstood by the so-called intellectualists or rationalists of the Absolute Idealistic variety. Practically the whole of the volume entitled *The Meaning of Truth* is devoted to the removal of these misunderstandings. And yet, as James himself admitted, that in part the misapprehensions were due to the glib manner in which such concepts as 'workability,' 'utility,' 'satisfactoriness,' 'cash-value,' etc. were used in the explication of the theory. It has been objected that the pragmatic theory of truth is primarily an appeal to action and ignores the theoretic interest, or that it cannot have a realistic epistemology and is shut up in solipsism, or that it explains not what truth is, but only how it is arrived at. James mentions how critics have caricatured the theory. He wrote:

"Not crediting us with that rudimentary insight, our critics treat our view as offering itself exclusively to engineers, doctors, financiers, and men of action generally, who need some sort of a rough and ready *weltanschauung,* but have no time or wit to study genuine philosophy. It is usually described as a characteristically American movement, a sort of bobtailed scheme of thought, excellently fitted for the man on the street, who naturally hates theory and wants cash returns immediately."[37]

The question is: How or by what method the *meaning* of truth is to be determined? Both the rationalists and the pragmatists accept that truth is a property of certain of our ideas, and that it means 'agreement' of our ideas with 'reality' and falsity means their 'disagreement' with reality. But what is meant by 'agreement' here and what is meant by 'reality' in this context? And here we find a divergence between the pragmatists and the anti-pragmatists. James is proposing a method called the 'pragmatic' method which is nothing other than that of tracing abstract concepts to their source in immediate 'pure experience.' The pragmatic method and the methodological postulate of referring concepts to immediate experience are *not* two separate things, though James failed to see this point clearly. This is, in effect, the descriptive phenomenological method which James followed in practice in solving dialectical difficulties. It is a reflective analysis of concepts in terms of their givenness in concrete experience. He judged the *adequacy* of a concept on the touchstone of its being discovered clearly in concrete experience. All *meanings* are to be located in experience through reflective articulation of it. Speaking of his pragmatic method as truly radical he wrote:

"He (the pragmatist) turns away from abstraction and insufficiency from verbal solutions, from bad a-priori reasons, from fixed principles, closed systems, pretended absolutes and origins. He turns towards *concreteness* and *adequacy,* towards *facts,* towards action and towards power. . . . It means the open air and possibilities of nature, as against dogma, artificiality, and pretence of finality in truth."[38]

That by "cash-value" he did not mean anything commercial or cheap pecuniary satisfaction or the gratification of a passing subjective whim, is evident from what he said about the intellectualist or absolutist treatment of such concepts as 'God,' 'Matter,' 'Reason,' 'The Absolute,' 'Energy,' etc. He said that all absolutist pettyfogging will vanish if we follow the pragmatic method in clarifying these concepts.

"You must bring out of each word its practical cash-value, set it at work within the *stream of your experience*"[39] (emphasis mine).

In the context of his method, James is asking, "What the word 'true' *means*, as applied to a statement";[40] what truth actually consists of.[41]

He says that the "truth-relation is a definitely experienceable relation, and therefore describable as well as nameable; that it is not unique in kind, and neither invariable nor universal."[42]

James' pragmatic answer to the question is that an idea or belief is *true* of a reality or thing when it *successfully* leads to it, actually or potentially, by a series of intermediary experiences and puts us in direct perceptual acquaintance with it. It is true when its *intention* is thus fulfilled. This is the only concrete experienceable *meaning* of the so-called 'agreement' of an idea with its object. Those theories which speak of a 'correspondence' between idea and reality subscribe to a 'copy-theory' of knowledge and truth, and regard 'reality' as something ready-made, and misconstrue the function of thought as mere imitation of it. All thinking, knowing and ideation is functional and instrumental. No mind entertains an idea unless it is actively *interested* in doing so, and when this interest in successfully ideating a thing is satisfied it is said to be a *true* idea. This interest and satisfaction have nothing to do with our subjective feelings, desires and impulses. It is cognitive interest that is meant here. There is no sense in speaking of truth-in-itself on the one hand, and 'reality' on the other, and then wonder how the former can agree with the latter. All these conundrums arise because of 'abstractionism' and a failure to bring the 'truth-relation' to its concreteness in immediate experience. Thus, he says, "The truth of an idea is not a stagnant property inherent in it. Truth *happens* to an idea. It *becomes* true, is *made* true by events. Its verity *is* in fact an event, a process, the process namely of its verifying itself, its verification. Its validity is the process of its *validation*."[43]

Again, "To agree in the widest sense with reality can only mean to be guided either straight up to it or into its surroundings, . . . Any idea that helps us to deal, whether practically or intellectually, with either the reality or its belongings, . . . that *fits,* in fact, and adapts our life to the reality's whole setting, will agree sufficiently to meet the requirement. It will be true of that reality."[44]

James affirms emphatically that the pragmatic theory of truth is 'epistemologically' realistic. It accepts the empirical reality independent of the knower. But it gives its own *meaning* to the concepts "knower" and "reality" in terms of 'pure experience' (although the very phrase, 'pure experience' is ambiguous) and does not artificially produce an initial hiatus between the two and then wonder how the 'twain shall meet.' He says:

"Truth here is a relation, not of our ideas to non-human realities, but of conceptual parts of our experience to sensational parts. Those thoughts are true which guide us to *beneficial interaction* with sensible particulars as they occur, whether they copy these in advance or not."[45]

James never denied the 'timeless truths' (?) of mathematics and logic. On the contrary he was aware of the nature of these alternative deductive systems based on selected axioms and spoke of these 'man-made objects' as necessary and eternal. He held that "relations of comparison are matters of direct inspection,"[46] and that the so-called 'eternal verities' of these ideal systems could be regarded as empirically true only when the 'ideal objects' were 'humanized' by being brought in relation with sensible facts.

James took great pains to repudiate the suggestion that the pragmatic theory of truth undermines the strictly *theoretic interest.* An idea is true theoretically when it *works for, satisfies* the theoretic motive. The human mind has found it most *useful* to build up and store great systems of theoretic nature, not for staring at them in lost admiration, but for their eventual use in concrete experiential interaction with reality. Here *consistency* is a sound principle only if its tentative and instrumental nature is recognized. He wrote:

"A true idea now means not only one that prepares us for an actual perception. It means also one that might prepare us for a merely possible perception. . . ."[47]

He regarded it as deliberate mischief on the part of the critics to think that when pragmatism spoke of 'satisfactoriness' it meant that an idea which is satisfactory is therefore true. It is *not* any kind of satisfaction which defines truth but a specific kind of satisfaction which is always determined by the logic of the cognitive situation.

Thus, knowledge, for James, in all its varieties arises from practical interests. It is rooted in an environment which it must understand and articulate. In its most preferred sense, knowledge by direct acquaintance is the best because it reveals the original and intrinsic nature of reality. But in most cases we have to be satisfied with conceptual knowledge or 'knowledge-about.' And the distinctive role and function of thought lies in giving us a grasp of the recurring and universal elements of reality so as to enable us to deal more effectively with sensible realities. To the extent that thought is able to do so 'satisfactorily' and 'successfully' it will be a true thought. In the clarification of all these concepts James has shown the efficacy of the method of reflective analysis of what is given in concrete cognitive experience.

Chapter IV

REALITY AND RATIONALITY

FROM the very beginning of his philosophical career, spanning over forty years, James had realized that the problem of 'reality' was inextricably bound up with that of the nature of 'rationality.' The history of philosophical thought has been concerned with the attainment of the most 'rational' conception of the universe or frame of things. The dichotomy of Reason and Experience has been a 'perennial' problem of philosophy since the time of Plato. The rationalists and the empiricists have attempted to come to grips with this problem in their own way. But the assumption underlying the historical protagonists of both rationalism and empiricism has been that whereas experience is concerned with the particular, the passing and the contingent phenomena, reason alone is capable of grasping 'reality' or 'being' which is universal, necessary and eternal. This assumed hiatus between experience and reason has dogged the philosophers ever since. The nature of experience has been misunderstood by the so-called empiricists, and the role of reason has been grossly misconstrued by the rationalists. Neither Plato, nor Descartes, Kant, Hegel or Husserl, to mention only a few, provided a thoroughgoing analysis of reason, either in terms of their own scientific level or from the perspective of a later period. All of them somehow assumed reason as a faculty of consciousness concerned with grasping 'being' or 'reality.' Contingent existence and experience were either dismissed as 'unreal' in the fashion of Plato, or regarded as 'mere' disorganized and chaotic matter for reason to introduce order and system *ab extra* à la Kant, or further still, rendered thoroughly rational as in the case of Hegel and Husserl (though in different ways). In other words, reason could grasp reality only through some sort of a 'rational experience' (dialectical in the case of Hegel, and viewed 'constitutively' in terms of pure essences in the case of Husserl). Thus, the problem was solved, or

49

'dissolved,' only by setting aside the particular and contingent facts of existence and experience and, in the case of Husserl, by 'purifying' experience through a series of 'reductions' following the *epoché*. W. James with his passion for the passing and the contingent could not follow this route. He had no patience with the pallor of such a 'purified' and 'distilled' experience. He insisted that we encounter and make contact with 'reality' in every kind of 'experience' and not merely in a rationally 'processed' one. He wrote this now famous line quoted earlier:

"Everything real must be experienceable somewhere, and every kind of thing experienced must somewhere be real."[1]

James, therefore, subjected the notion of 'rationality' to a thorough phenomenological analysis as early as 1879 in his famous essay, "Sentiment of Rationality"[2] and adumbrated the gist of his later chapter, "The Perception of Reality" (*The Principles of Psychology*, vol. II, 1890) in a very early essay, "Remarks on Spencer's Definition of Mind as Correspondence,"[3] published in 1878. These twin concepts of 'reality' and 'rationality' have dominated his psychology, epistemology and philosophy of religion. Before we proceed to examine these concepts, a few brief remarks are called for on the question: Is there only one James or are there several? On this question R. B. Perry, James' student and valued colleague, wrote: "There is one and only one James from the beginning to the end."[4]

Others have thought that one can discern several unharmonized strands in James, such as his radical empiricism, pragmatism, logical realism, naturalism, and later supernaturalism and even mysticism. The task of harmonizing these so-called various strands is a hopeless one if one does not grasp the dominant idea in James' philosophy. Perry is essentially right in holding that such a germinal idea in James is "the essentially active and interested character of the human mind."[4a] This dynamic and teleological character of the human mind was set forth by James in the essay, "Remarks on Spencer's Definition of Mind as Correspondence" published in 1878, which has been referred to above. Perry is also of the opinion that even when James, in his later works, wrote sympathetically of religious experiences, mysticism, immortality and 'psychical research,' he never forgot his early naturalistic position. We shall find below that this is a controversial interpretation. Here I wish to account for and explain the inherent tension in James' philosophy between his 'naturalistic realism' and the alleged 'supernaturalism,' 'voluntarism,' and 'experientialism' in his various works. This tension is inevitable in all philosophies which make 'experience' their point of departure and understand, as James rightly did, the dynamic and interested character of the human mind. With this point of departure all reality can only be 'experienced' reality in which the active human mind plays a significant role. Unless, therefore one has a proper concept of experience and understands its natural, socio-historical and cultural context, one is apt to land in a completely subjective philosophy, as did Husserl.

James' early training in philosophy, evolutionary biology and his thorough acquaintance with experimental method helped him to give 'experience' a footing in nature and adopt a 'methodological pluralism' in philosophizing. And yet this is bound to be a tightrope walking, and one may slip from naturalism to 'pure experientialism.' As a matter of fact, James' openness to all kinds of 'experience' such as religious, mystical, 'psychical,' etc. could be understood on the basis of his concepts of 'rationality' and 'reality' which he adopted from the very beginning of his philosophical career. In these concepts, the role of the 'total' character of the experiencing Ego with its cognitive, emotional and volitional aspects played a decisive role. If one emphasizes only this latter aspect of his philosophy, one could interpret it as 'philosophical anthropology' as the current jargon goes. But, as we shall see below, James never completely lost sight of his footing in naturalism, and he regarded sense-experience and knowledge of sense-objects as the prototype and paradigm of all knowledge and reality. Even the 'psychical,' religious and 'mystical' experiences were to be regarded as authentic only when they had the character of sense-experience with its 'compelling' quality. We have already said in earlier chapters that his 'pragmatism' and 'radical empiricism' were not two, but one principle methodologically speaking, with the help of which James traced the *meaning* of all concepts phenomenologically to their givenness in immediate experience. Hence, it will not be far too wrong to say with Perry that from the very beginning there was only one James *but* with the modification that he had a dual potentiality inherent in his position. He developed both of them, sometimes emphasizing one, sometimes the other, thus giving the impression of an uneasy balance to many readers.

What then is the criterion of reality and rationality? James is attempting a phenomenological analysis of these concepts in terms of 'felt' experience. The key idea to the whole problem is found in James' early essay "Remarks on Spencer's Definition of Mind as Correspondence" (1878). It appears that the bulk of his later works on psychology, philosophy, and theory of knowledge is an elaboration of that basic idea. He gave a scathing criticism there of Spencer's account of mind as a 'mere' correspondence of internal relations to 'outer reality' and repudiated outright such a passive role of mind as mere 'duplication' of outer nature. He asked the question: What is Reality? and suggested that in answering it not only our cognitive interests but also our active, emotional, aesthetic and religious interests ought to be kept in view. He concluded that essay with:

"I, for my part, cannot escape the consideration, . . . that the Knower is not simply a mirror floating with no foot-hold anywhere, and passively reflecting an order that he comes upon and finds simply existing. The Knower is an actor, and co-efficient of the truth on one side, whilst on the other he registers the truth which he helps to create. Mental interests, hypotheses, postulates, so far as they are bases for human action—action which to a great extent transforms the world—help to *make* the truth which they declare. In other words, there belongs to mind, from its birth upward, a spontaneity, a vote. It is in the game, and not a mere looker-on; and its judgments of the *should-be,* its ideals, cannot be peeled off from the body of the *cogitandum* as if they were excrescences, or meant, at most survival. We know so little about the ultimate nature of things, or of ourselves, that it would be sheer folly dogmatically to say that an ideal rational order may not be real. *The only objective criterion of reality is coerciveness, in the long run, over thought* (emphasis mine). Objective facts, Spencer's outward relations, are real only because they coerce sensation. Any interest which should be coercive on the same massive scale would be *eodem jure* real. By its very essence, the reality of a thought is proportionate to the way it grasps us. *Its intensity, its seriousness—its interest, in a word*

—taking these qualities, not at any given instant, but as shown by the total upshot of experience (emphasis mine). If judgments of the *should-be* are fated to grasp us in this way, they are what "correspond."[5]

In this significant passage James is aware of a possible 'subjectivistic' misinterpretation of the descriptive criteria of the reality of thought in terms of its 'grasping' power, its intensity, seriousness and interest. These are 'experienced' characteristics but what guarantee is there that these may not be illusory? To obviate such a criticism James adds the phrase, "taking these qualities, not at any given instant, but as shown by the total upshot of experience." Here James is implying that in order to correct 'illusory' experience we have to subject it to the discipline of a cumulatively appraised reflective criticism. But that is still an experience, though a reflective one. We can therefore never pass out of felt 'experience' to judge whether it is real or illusory.

By what criteria then are we to judge the 'rationality' of a philosophical conception of reality? What does it *mean* to have a rational conception of the universe? How does it 'feel' to have a rational conception of the nature of things? In this phenomenological inquiry James is attempting to describe how rationality 'presents' itself in immediately felt experience—what its essential structure is. He says:

"A strong feeling of ease, peace, rest, is one of them. The transition from a state of puzzle and perplexity to rational comprehension is full of lively relief and pleasure."[6]

Again:

"This feeling of sufficiency of the present moment, of its absoluteness—this absence of all need to explain it, account for it, or justify it, is what I call the Sentiment of Rationality. As soon, in short, as we are enabled from any cause whatever to think with perfect fluency, the thing we think of seems to us *protanto* rational."[7]

James then goes on to discuss how this felt experience of 'ease and sufficiency' is manifested on the theoretical as well as the practical planes of human experience. If a conception of the Cosmos is to be 'felt' as rational on the theoretic plane it should strike a balance between two seemingly opposed human passions—the pas-

sion for unifying and simplifying the sensible diversity of phenomena under a single principle, and the rival passion for a detailed
discrimination of particulars and unceasing "loyalty to clearness
and integrity of perception, dislike of blurred outlines, of vague
identifications, etc."[8]

An overemphasis on one or the other will not be 'felt' as a completely 'rational' universe. A bare principle of abstract universality
which drops the particulars of sense-experience will not be 'experienced' as the sought-after Ultimate Principle of Intelligibility. This
is the weakness in all Absolutistic Philosophies such as those of
Spinoza, Hegel, Advaita Vedanta etc. On the contrary, a universe
thought to be composed of only discrete, disconnected and chaotic
particulars will be 'felt' as the most irrational one. James points
out that Hegel's unification in the Absolute Spirit does not satisfy
the sentiment of rationality because the 'brute fact' as something
given in experience cannot be absorbed in the Hegelian Absolute.
He says:

"The philosopher's logical tranquility is thus in essence no other
than the boor's."[9]

He then goes on to consider whether mystic ecstasy or rapture
is able to produce that 'peace and ease' of rationality and says that
such an experience has lacked universality and at its best, is limited to only a few persons, and is, therefore, not able to satisfy the
sentiment of rationality of most persons. He concludes his remarks
about theoretic rationality by saying:

"Existence then will be a brute fact to which as a whole the
emotion of ontologic wonder shall rightly cleave, but remain eter-
nally unsatisfied."[10]

This passage shows James' concern for natural facts of existence
which function as a constant backdrop to man's experience.

Turning from 'unsatisfied' theoretic rationality to the quest for
'practical rationality' James emphasizes the role of the dynamic and
active powers of the human mind on this issue. Here again the
question is: What does it 'feel' like to experience rationality in
practical life? In other words, if two rival conceptions of reality
are equally fitted to satisfy logical or theoretic demands, what criteria will settle the issue of their rationality? James answers by

saying that in such a case, that conception which fulfills our active and emotional impulses and satisfies the aesthetic demands will be deemed as more rational. He points out that man is most concerned about his *future*. Our mind has an inveterate sense of futurity or expectancy, and the emotional effect of settled expectancy is immense. He therefore says:

"For a philosophy to succeed on a universal scale it must define the future *congruously with our spontaneous powers.*"[11] In order that a philosophic conception may be experienced as rational it should not "baffle and disappoint our dearest desires and most cherished powers," and it should give our intimate powers an "object to press against," and these powers must be felt to be relevant in universal affairs. In particular, the ultimate principle of such a conception should 'legitimate' our emotions of fortitude, hope, rapture, admiration, earnestness, etc. Having armed himself with such a criterion, he brings in *faith* as one of the human powers which he thinks must be included in any conception of a rational universe. In this essay as well as in his "The Will to Believe" and, "Is Life Worth Living?" he attempts to show how faith is an important element in every department of life such as science, morals, and religion. In questions about God, Immortality, free-will and moral order, "faith creates its own verification." He concludes this chapter by saying that *in addition* to meeting logical demands a philosophy to be rational should: (i) settle expectancy and our sense of futurity; (ii) make an appeal to all our higher powers, (iii) and make room for *faith* in matters where it is relevant.

From the above account it appears that James toned down the criterion of rationality by a strong dose of elements of emotional needs, active powers and lastly, faith. The flood gates were opened and James found himself inundated by all kinds of 'religious' experiences, mysticisms, 'psychical' experiences, etc. One wonders whether such a generous compromise with active and emotional human powers may not have so diluted the rigour of rationality as to throw the pendulum back to the other extreme. But James assures us that 'facts of nature,' theoretic consistency and satisfaction of our active and emotional powers are equally important in deciding whether a philosophic conception is rational or not.[12] Up to the very last James maintained a 'composite' view of 'rationality.' He realized the elements of 'rationality' and 'irrationality' as it were, in a Hegelian conception of the Absolute. He wrote:

"Probably the weightiest contribution to our feeling of the universe which the notion of the absolute brings is the assurance that however disturbed the surface may be, at bottom all is well with the cosmos–central peace abiding at the heart of endless agitation. This conception is rational in many ways, beautiful aesthetically, beautiful intellectually . . . , and beautiful morally, if the enjoyment of security can be accounted moral. *Practically it is less beautiful; for . . . in representing the deepest reality of the world as static and without a history, it loosens the world's hold upon our sympathies and leaves the soul of it foreign.*"[13]

Rejecting a purely intellectualistic[14] criterion of rationality as one-sided and recognizing the difficulty of the practical task of reconciling the various competing criteria of rationality he wrote:

"But rationality has at least four dimensions: intellectual, aesthetic, moral and practical; *and to find a world rational to the maximum degree in all these respects simultaneously is no easy matter*"[15] (emphasis mine).

"The rationality we gain in one coin we thus pay for in another; and the problem accordingly seems at first sight to resolve itself into that of getting a conception which will yield the largest *balance* of rationality rather than one which will yield perfect rationality of every description."[16]

Having discussed James' analysis of 'rationality' we turn to his treatment of 'reality.' Both of these concepts are two aspects of the same coin, and James' chapter on "The Perception of Reality" in *The Principles of Psychology,* vol. II, 1890, is an elaboration of his earlier views on the topic discussed above. He discusses the problem in two ways–(i) a phenomenological analysis of the nature or structure of our experience of reality (ii) and its history or the conditions of production and its connection with other facts. We are mainly concerned with the former. He says:

". . . belief or the sense of reality, is a sort of feeling more allied to the emotions than to anything else."[17]

He regards this 'sense' of reality as *sui generis*. It is a psychic attitude and is more than the mere 'thought' of an object. He recommends in this connection Brentano's distinction between conception (judgment) and belief. Mere 'thought' of the object, simple or complex, may exist without belief, but belief always presupposes 'thought.' What then, are the conditions or circumstances under which such a 'feel' or 'experience' of reality of an object arises? James says:

"The sense that anything we think of is unreal can only come, then, when that thing is contradicted by some other thing of which we think. *Any object which remains uncontradicted is ipso facto believed and posited as absolute reality.*"[18]

In our experience of 'reality' the Ego plays an important part and "every object we think of gets at last referred to one world or another. . . ."[19]

Though James recognized the paramount reality of the world of sense-experience to the very last, he admitted various other orders of reality in his conception of the total universe such as the world of 'scientific realities'; of 'ideal relations' or abstract truths expressed in "logical, mathematical, metaphysical, ethical, or aesthetic propositions"; of "illusions and prejudices common to the race"; of various 'supernatural realities' such as the Christian Heaven and Hell, mythology, etc.; the various worlds of individual opinion; and the worlds of sheer madness and vagary. It is difficult to reconcile the various pronouncements of James on this problem of the rival claims of these different sub-universes. And yet the guiding thread which binds them all together and entitles them to be regarded as 'real' is their *active relation* to the Ego. He says:

"For, in the strict and ultimate sense of the word existence, everything which can be thought of at all exists as *some* sort of object, whether mythical object, individual thinker's object, or object in outer space, and for intelligence at large. Errors, fictions, tribal beliefs, are parts of the whole great universe which God has made, and He must have meant all these things to be in it, each in its respective place."[20]

And:

"*In the relative sense, . . . , reality means simply relations to our emotional and active life. . . . In this sense, whatever excites and stimulates our interest is real;* whenever an object so appeals to us that we turn to it, accept it, fill our mind with it, or practically take account of it, so far it is real for us, and we believe it. Whenever . . . we ignore it, fail to consider it or act upon it, despise it, reject it, forget it, so far it is unreal for us and disbelieved."[21]

He continues:

"The *fons et origo of all reality, whether from the absolute or the practical point of view, is thus subjective, is ourselves.* As bare logical thinkers, without emotional reaction, we give reality to whatever objects we think of, for they are really phenomena, or objects of our passing thought, if nothing more. But *as thinkers with emotional reaction, we give what seems to us a still higher degree of reality to whatever things we select and emphasize and turn to with a will.* These are *living* realities."[22]

And:

"The world of living realities as contrasted with unrealities is thus anchored in the Ego, considered as an active and emotional term. That is the hook from which the rest dangles, the absolute support."[23]

These passages might be interpreted to suggest that, for James, the criterion of reality is purely 'subjective' landing us in a kind of 'solipsism.' And yet James assures us that the word 'Ego' is used here in the way common sense does without prejudice to its further analysis. Therefore, if these passages are read out of connection with the rest of his thought they might suggest the position of a subjective idealist. But if they are interpreted in the light of his analysis of 'Ego' or Self and in the background of his essays on "Radical Empiricism" and "Does Consciousness Exist?" it will be possible to avoid such a misconstruction. That James' language here is ambiguous there is no doubt. Moreover, even if the Ego is interpreted in the way James wants us to do, it is difficult to avoid the impression that James' overemphasis on the role of the active Ego jeopardizes the independent existence of natural events which antedate human experience, both individually and collectively. Time and again, however, James points out the paramount reality of sensible objects. He says:

"Sensible objects are thus either our realities or the tests of our own realities. Conceived objects must show sensible effects or else be disbelieved."[24]

And:

"No mere floating conception, no mere disconnected rarity, ever displaces vivid things or permanent things from our belief. A conception, to prevail, must terminate in the world of orderly sensible experience."[25]

And yet the heart of the problem is to distinguish between the 'perceived object' and the independently 'existing object' of the natural world. This will require a more adequate analysis of the concept of 'object' than James has succeeded in doing. He nevertheless recognizes that the fundamental questions of what this stirring, exciting power, this interest consists in, which some objects have, and which are those intimate relations with our life which give reality, cannot be answered easily in an offhand manner. Limiting himself to an analysis of our sense of 'experienced reality' he admits the reality of 'Spiritualistic' phenomena, when he says:

"But one who has actually seen such a phenomenon, under what seems to him sufficiently 'test-conditions,' will hold to his sensible experience through thick and thin, even though the whole fabric of 'science' should be rent in twain. . . . But the spirit which animates him is that on which ultimately the very life and health of Science rest."[26]

The above passage is a tautology with the phrase "what seems to him sufficiently 'test-conditions'" retained as important qualification. But the crucial question is: Are what *seem* to one observer as 'test-conditions' *really* so for all other equally competent observers? Here, experimental method and intersubjective checking are important aids in deciding the issue. This shows how perilously near James is to the charmed circle of 'subjectivism' on his criterion of *our* 'sense' of reality. Equipped with his own definition of 'rationality' it is easy for him to say that:

"That theory will be most generally believed which, besides offering us objects able to account satisfactorily for our sensible experience, also offers those which are most interesting, those which appeal most urgently to our aesthetic, emotional, and active needs."[27]

With this passage, the criteria of 'rationality' and 'reality' coalesce and the circle is complete. James, as he progressed in his philosophical career, emphasized more and more these active, emotional and dynamic needs of man in determining what is real and what is not. Gradually, his early robust and healthy naturalism recedes in the background and 'supernaturalism' occupies him more and more. He admitted that, "Materialistic, or so-called 'scientific' conceptions of the universe have so far gratified the purely intellectual interests more than the mere sentimental conceptions have."[28] But, he continues, . . . "they leave the emotional and active interests cold. The perfect object of belief would be a God or a 'Soul of the World,' represented both optimistically and moralistically (if such a combination could be), and withal so definitely conceived as to show us why our phenomenal experiences should be sent to us by Him in just the very way in which they come. All Science and all History would thus be accounted for in the deepest and simplest fashion."[29]

And:

"It is safe to say that, if ever such a system is satisfactorily excogitated, mankind will drop all other systems and cling to that one alone as real."[30]

In the light of these passages and others in his *A Pluralistic Universe* it is difficult to support the thesis of R. B. Perry that there is only one James throughout. In later years, James' interests in religious experiences, psychical research and immortality gave way to his early naturalism. He was influenced more and more by Bergson and Fechner's conception of 'a great reservoir' in which the memories of the earth's inhabitants are pooled and preserved." He wrote:

"There are resources in us that naturalism with its literal and legal virtues never recks of, possibilities that take our breath away, of another kind of happiness and power, based on giving up our own will and and letting something higher work for us, and these seem to show a world wider than either physics or philistine ethics can imagine."[31]

Again:

"The believer (religious) is continuous, to his own consciousness at any rate, with a wider self from which saving experiences flow in."[32]

Basing his views of reality on his studies in descriptive psychology, religious experiences, psychical research and the thoughts of Fechner and Bergson, James exhorted his readers:

"To accept, along with the superhuman consciousness, the notion that it is not all-embracing, the notion, in other words, that there is a God, but that he is finite, either in power or in knowledge, or in both at once."[33]

He labeled his universe as 'multiverse' and called his system of reality "the thicker and the more radical empiricism."[34] He expressed the formula for his 'multiverse' as "Ever not quite" and said, "Things are 'with' one another in many ways, but nothing includes everything."[35]

In his *Varieties of Religious Experience* (1902) James preferred to call himself a "supernaturalist" but not of the refined or universalistic type, but of the 'piecemeal' variety.

The former, according to him,

"surrenders, . . . , too easily to naturalism. It takes the facts of physical science at their face value, and leaves the laws of life just as naturalism finds them, with no hope of remedy, in case their fruits are bad."[36]

But, says James, he believes in 'piecemeal' supernaturalism in which, "there is a wider world of being than that of our everyday consciousness," "there are forces whose effects on us are intermittent," and "one facilitating condition of the effects is the openness of the 'subliminal' door."[37]

He says:

"I am so impressed by the importance of these phenomena that I adopt the hypothesis which they so naturally suggest. At these places at least, I say, it would seem as though transmundane energies, God, if you will, produced immediate effects within the natural world to which the rest of our experience belongs."[38]

It should not be forgotten that James at one time took nitrous oxide gas himself and wrote many sentences under its intoxication.[39] As a consequence he revised his views on Hegel's Absolute and completely toned down his earlier radically critical views on it. Only six months before his death in 1910 he described his own four 'mystical' experiences and put forward a suggestion that, "states of mystical intuition may be only very sudden and great extensions of the ordinary 'field of consciousness,' "[40] and that the extension consists in "an immense spreading of the margin of the field, so that knowledge ordinarily transmarginal would become included, and the ordinary margin would grow more central."[41]

Further:

"My hypothesis is that a movement of the threshold downwards will similarly bring a mass of subconscious memories, conceptions, emotional feelings, and perceptions of relation etc. into view all at once; and that if this enlargement of the nimbus that surrounds the sensational present is vast enough, while no one of the items it contains attracts our attention singly, we shall have the conditions fulfilled for a kind of consciousness in all essential respects like that termed mystical. It will be transient, if the change of threshold is transient. *It will be of reality, enlargement, and illumination,* possibly rapturously so. It will be of unification, for the present coalesces in it with the ranges of the remote quite out of its reach under ordinary circumstances; and the sense of *relation* will be greatly enhanced. Its form will be intuitive or perceptual, not conceptual . . ."[42] (emphasis mine).

From this passage it appears that James is giving a 'naturalistic description of 'mystical states' in terms of the fact-revealed sense of reality together with the perceptual form of the experience. His explanation that such experiences are enlargements of the margin of our ordinary consciousness sounds less supernaturalistic than the earlier passages quoted above from *The Varieties of Religious Experience* when he called himself a supernaturalist of the 'piecemeal' type. In the light of all these passages might it not be nearer the truth to say that despite James' extreme 'openness' and sensitivity to all kinds of experience the pull of his early naturalism schooled in the scientific disciplines of physiology and medicine was effective till the very last? The genius of James defies rigid classificatory and Either/Or labels. He evinced in his works a vast range and richness of experience coupled with a rare analytical skill in describing their essential structures with unequalled ease and felicity. His philosophy of experience, according to our presentation above, may with justification be called phenomenological in its *main* aspects. It will not be far too wrong to regard him as a powerful precursor of an American brand of naturalistic and realistic phenomenology.

One can discern an 'implicit' *epoché* in his descriptive analysis of experience in as much as he had to adopt a reflective attitude of detachment in order to reveal the essential *meaning* of subjectivity (self), objectivity, reality, truth, knowledge, rationality, etc. His methodological pluralism saved him from becoming a 'pure' phenomenologist of the subjectivistic type. His theory of 'pure experience' was not akin to the 'purity' of consciousness attained by Husserl through various 'reductions.' Its purity lay in its being *antecedent* to all reflective activities—in being a mere 'that' which when reflected upon gave rise to the distinction of 'subject' and 'object.' His theory of 'intentionality' of consciousness did not 'bracket out' real objects as Husserl had done. Knowledge was of "real objects" and not of 'intentional' objects only. And his critical examination of the nature of 'consciousness,' as well as his emphasis on the role of the body in all experiences gave his phenomenology a different flavor from that of many others and saved him from being trapped in the lion's den of subjectivism.

Section B

JOHN DEWEY

Chapter V

TOWARD A NATURALISTIC PHENOMENOLOGY OF EXPERIENCE

IN the preceding chapters I have interpreted William James as a *precursor* of an American brand of Naturalistic phenomenology of experience. Though in later years he became interested in religious experiences of all types (including mystical) and lent his massive support to a sympathetic study of 'psychical' experiences, yet he never wholly gave up his early naturalistic and realistic standpoint.[a] His concept of 'pure experience' though ambiguous, bore testimony to the freshness and inimitable genius of this great individual. 'Pure experience' was to be understood in two contexts. First, in the context of our experience of continuity and flux as opposed to Humean dismemberment of it into disparate and atomistic perceptions and impressions. Secondly, in the context of a 'materia prima,' a 'naif immediacy' where the distinctions of the 'that' and the 'what,' subject and object had not yet arisen. In this sense it stood for 'reality' or 'nature' which Dewey was to elaborate later. James equivocated in making his meaning clear on this aspect and denied that it stood for any monistic and metaphysical 'stuff.' He wrote:

"There are as many stuffs as there are 'natures' in the things experienced. If you ask what one bit of experience is made of, the answer is always the same: 'It is made of *that,* of just what appears, of space, of intensity, of flatness, brownness, heaviness, or what not."[1]

Here then, experience was only a "collective name for all these sensible natures."

When we come to Dewey we find a naturalistic phenomenology of experience become almost fully articulate and self-conscious. To associate the name of Dewey with 'phenomenology' might shock the scholarly sensitivity of many so-called phenomenological 'purists.' But the fact is that without mentioning this name Dewey was using a descriptive-phenomenological method for an analysis of the generic structures of experience. He called this method naturalistic empiricism in his Carus Lectures published under the title of *Experience and Nature*. A careful reading of James and Dewey will show that except for his indifference to James' interests in religious and 'psychical' phenomena, the only philosopher who fully grasped the method and the thrust of James' philosophy was John Dewey. Dewey was quick to realize the revolutionary potentiality of an appeal to 'immediate experience' in criticizing traditional dualisms of mind and body, subject and object, experience and reason, value and existence, form and matter, etc., etc. He regarded James' *Principles of Psychology* as a major contribution in two ways—one, in conceiving of consciousness or experience as a continuous stream and thus ending the dualism of mind and body; second, in conceiving the mind as dynamic, active, interested, and selective. Dewey wrote that here we have a:

". . . re-interpretation of introspective psychology in which James denies that sensations, images and ideas are discrete and in which he replaces them by a continuous stream which he calls the 'stream of consciousness.' This conception necessitates a consideration of relations as an immediate part of the field of consciousness, having the same status as qualities."[2]

Again he said that:

"Long ago I learned from William James that there are immediate experiences of the connections linguistically expressed by conjunctions and prepositions. My doctrinal position is but a generalization of what is involved in this fact."[3]

It is therefore safe to aver that explicitly and implicitly Dewey conceived of the philosophic method, after the style of James, as a phenomenological description of immediate experience. All concepts and ideas were to be traced back to and tested at the bar of primary experience to find out, as it were, their 'cash-value' or 'pragmatic equivalent' (in the graphic phraseology of James). It was with reference to such primary experience or direct non-reflective experience that the old philosophical puzzles arising out of non-empirical and transcendental methods could be dissolved. Dewey conceived of this immediate experience as pre-reflective, primary, and ultimate. It will be our endeavor, in what follows, to bring out the meaning of such an immediate experience in Dewey's thought. Dewey was certainly aware of the difficulty of reaching and describing such an immediate experience without the use of rational categories and without the introduction of a selective bias. He understood, as James did, "the contrast between gross, macroscopic, crude subject-matters in primary experience and the refined, derived objects of reflection."[4] But he pointed out that those who followed non-empirical methods in philosophizing failed to refer back the products of reflective inquiry to primary, immediate experience for verification. Not only this, they failed to grasp the function of such ideas and concepts of reflective inquiry. Instead of understanding their function of clarifying and enriching our primary experience, and thus giving us an added meaning and control over them, they set these concepts as antecedent realities in their own right. This was, what James called, the fallacy of vicious abstractionism. Dewey named this procedure 'the philosophic fallacy.' He wrote:

"Selective emphasis, choice, is inevitable whenever reflection occurs. This is not an evil. Deception comes only when the presence and operation of choice is concealed, disguised, denied. Empirical method finds and points to the operation of choice as it does to any other event. *Thus it protects us from conversion of eventual functions into antecedent existence:* a conversion that may be said to be *the* philosophic fallacy, whether it be performed in behalf of mathematical subsistences, esthetic essences, the purely physical order of nature, or God"[5] (emphasis mine).

Dewey designated this method as 'denotative'[6] in so far as it relies on a direct appeal to what is revealed in immediate experience. It is a call to 'seeing' free from all rationalistic bias and presuppositions. He wrote:

"An empirical finding is refuted, not by denial that one finds things to be thus and so, *but by giving directions for a course of experience that results in finding its opposite to be the case.* To convince of error as well as to lead to truth is *to assist another to see* and find something which he hitherto has failed to find and recognize"[7] (emphasis mine).

Here a formal resemblance to E. Husserl's procedure is evident, but there is an enormous material difference in so far as, whereas Husserl was concerned with a descriptive analysis of essential structures of our acts of experiencing (having performed the *epoché* and 'bracketed out' the natural world), Dewey was endeavoring to get at the back of all reflective analyses and to point out 'denotatively' generic structure of gross, primary experience in terms of an active interaction between a dynamic organism and a changing natural and social environment. No wonder he (Dewey) arrived at a different view of primary experience than did Husserl. Dewey realized the enormous difficulty of such an enterprise when he said:

"But this experience is already overlaid and saturated with the products of the reflection of past generations and by-gone ages. It is filled with interpretations, classifications, due to sophisticated thought, which have become incorporated into what seems to be fresh, naive empirical material."[8]

However, he did not think the task to be a hopeless one and believed that a genuinely descriptive philosophy could be called upon to perform such a critique of past 'prejudices.' He wrote:

"These incorporated results of past reflection, *welded into the genuine materials of first-hand experience,* may become organs of enrichment if they are detected and reflected upon"[9] (emphasis mine).

Again:

"We cannot achieve recovery of primitive naiveté. But there is attainable a cultivated naiveté of eye, ear and thought, one that can be acquired only through the discipline of severe thought."[10]

At this stage, it will be relevant to point out a significant feature of Dewey's method. His appeal to primary experience was one to the immediacy of non-reflective experience and yet he was shrewd enough to recognize that *all* notions of experience were products of social and intellectual factors which affect the very quality of experience undergone. Therefore there was no pretense of starting from 'scratch' in an *absolutely* presuppositionless manner in the style of Husserl.[10(a)] Husserl was attempting to do the impossible by 'bracketing' out everything including the products of socio-historical and intellectual factors from any consideration of pure experiential structures. We have noticed above that such an attempt, however awe-inspiring in its rationalistic vision, was bound to fail and this accounted for the subjectivistic turn in Husserl's later philosophy. In contrast, both James and Dewey, though they talked of immediate gross experience, did not commit what Marvin Farber has called the "fallacy of illicit ignorance." Both of them thoroughly learned and assimilated the meaning and significance of the new biology (and the new psychology based on it) as well as the experimental method of inquiry. Dewey, in his notion of experience lay his finger on the basic category of the "interaction of organism and environment, resulting in some adaptation which secures utilization of the latter."[11]

No matter at what level and at what historical period experience is considered it is always a product of a 'transaction' between a live organism and a changing natural and social environment. The content of experience might change according to changing social and intellectual factors but the *generic pattern and structure* of it shows the same pervasive features which Dewey attempted to describe. And yet this social and historical determination of experience could not be used self-referentially to discredit Dewey's own notion of experience because the generic category of 'transaction' applies equally to all socio-historical periods and is a pervasive one. Moreover, this 'transaction' is not merely an uncritical assumption. Dewey himself was an unremitting critic of all such assumptions. He, consistently with his descriptive-empirical method, invited all to confirm the transactional nature of experience in their own experiences.

Before we proceed to analyze Dewey's notion of immediate experience it will be proper to ask whether and in what sense Dewey's philosophy of experience is naturalistic and not subjectivistic. Anyone who begins with experience is bound to face the problem of subjectivism because the word 'experience' has mentalistic and subjectivistic connotation and overtones. Santayana[12] branded Dewey's naturalism as 'half-hearted and short-winded' and indicted it of showing 'the dominance of the foreground' in the sense that in his system the foreground of Experience with its 'local' perspective was supposed to but could not do justice to the infinite nature of Nature which antedates all human experience and existence. Dewey was aware of this possible misinterpretation of his notion of experience and took special care to remove it. He himself criticized the older empiricists' identification of experience with the subject's *acts of experiencing* and pointed out that these acts of experiencing were arrived at by a reflective analysis of only one aspect of total experience "to the deliberate omission, *for the purpose of the inquiry in hand,* of *what* is experienced."[13] He wrote:

"Reflective analysis of one element in actual experience is undertaken; its result is then taken to be primary; as a consequence the subject-matter of actual experience from which the analytic result was derived is rendered dubious and problematic, although it is assumed at every step of the analysis. Genuine empirical method sets out from actual subject-matter of primary experience, recognizes that reflection discriminates a new factor in it, the *act* of seeing, makes an object of that, and then uses that new object, the organic response to light, to regulate, when needed, further experiences of the subject-matter already contained in primary experience."[14]

Dewey regards the former procedure to be the heart of all '*subjectivisms.*'[15]

Dewey conceived experience to be capable of revealing the nature of Nature. He wrote:

"Experience is not a veil that shuts man off from nature; it is a means of penetrating continually further into the heart of nature."[16]

Again:

". . . experience, if scientific inquiry is justified, is no infinitesimally thin layer of foreground of nature, but that it penetrates into it, reaching down into its depths, and in such a way that its grasp is capable of expansion; . . . unless we are prepared to deny all validity to scientific inquiry, these facts have a value that cannot be ignored for the general theory of the relation of nature and experience."[17]

He recognised that experience was a late comer in the cosmic history of nature, and yet, "when experience does occur, no matter at what limited portion of time and space, it enters into possession of some portion of nature and in such a manner as to render other of its precincts accessible."[18]

Thus, for Dewey, the twin conceptions of nature and experience are intimately interrelated. Experience in all of its varieties–including the ordinary gross one, scientific, moral and esthetic–reveals the nature of Nature. These are culminations of nature but do not exhaust the infinite potentialities of nature conceived as background. There is no harm in speaking of experience as the foreground, provided it is recognised that this foreground is capable of penetrating in a cumulative and progressive manner the infinitely rich hinterland of nature. Santayana was misinterpreting Dewey in accusing him of 'cosmic impiety' in identifying the foreground with the background of nature. We shall see in a later chapter how Dewey's concept of experience was enriched in his theory of art as developed by him in his classic *Art as Experience*. He was keenly and sensitively aware of the fact that however far back we push our analysis, experience always has that ever-receding horizon encompassing it—that ever-widening fringe, that context, that aura of something beyond and bigger than ourselves—that feel of the 'More' which we call the Universe. To accentuate this feeling, to arouse this sense of unity through shared experience is the great function of art. As Dewey puts it:

"But however broad the field, it is still felt as not the whole; the margins shade into that indefinite expanse beyond which imagination calls the Universe. This sense of the including whole implicit in ordinary experience is rendered intense within the frame of a painting or a poem. It, rather than any special purgation is that which reconciles us to the events of tragedy."[19]

Again:

"A work of art elicits and accentuates this quality of being a whole and of belonging to the larger, all inclusive whole which is the universe in which we live."[20]

In one of the most celebrated passages Dewey brings out this close interconnection between experience and nature. He says:

". . . experience is *of* as well as *in* nature. It is not experience which is experienced, but nature—stones, plants, animals, diseases, health, temperature, electricity, and so on. Things interacting in certain ways *are* experience; they are what is experienced. . . . Experience thus reaches down into nature; it has depth. It also has breadth and to an indefinitely elastic extent, it stretches. That stretch constitutes inference."[21]

The distinction Dewey makes between "gross, macroscopic, crude, subject-matters in primary experience and the refined, derived objects of reflection"[22] is basic to the understanding of his entire philosophic thought. In the integral unity of primary experience 'things' are "had"[22(a)] for use and enjoyment. When the data of primary experience are inquired into for any purpose in a specific context, they give rise to *objects* of reflection. The objects of science and philosophy belong to this latter class. This reflective inquiry enlarges and enriches the *meaning* of primary data of immediate experience. "They become means of control, of enlarged use and enjoyment of ordinary things."[23]

It is because 'experience' is a double-barrelled word Dewey recalls James' use of this phrase in the latter's *Essays in Radical Empiricism* that philosophers have confused between the primary inclusive integrity of it and the objects of reflective inquiry. In its primary sense, experience is what it is–an occurrence in which there are as yet no divisions of "act and material, subject and object" but only "an unanalyzed totality."[24] 'Things' and 'thoughts' refer "to products discriminated by reflection out of primary experience."[25] All theories of experience which identify it exclusively with the *acts* of experiencing in isolation from the 'things' experienced are committing the fallacy of vicious intellectualism and abstractionism because what are simply partial products of reflective inquiry are mistakenly taken for the whole of experience. This leads to the conception of experience as "subjective private consciousness set over against nature."[26]

For Dewey, not only primary experience but consciousness (reflective experience) too is *intentional*–but at different levels. Primary experience is of qualitied existential 'things' or rather 'events' which are 'had' within an inclusive transactional situation. These very 'events' when inquired into become 'objects' of conscious awareness or reflective experience. Events and objects are not two different things because "objects are events *with* meanings; tables, the milky way, chairs, stars, cats, dogs, electrons, ghosts, centaurs, historic epochs and all the infinitely multifarious subject-matter of discourse designable by common nouns, verbs and their qualifiers."[27]

It will be fruitful to compare and contrast Husserl's concept of *intentionality* with that of Dewey. There is no evidence to show that Dewey and Husserl ever read each other's works. And yet it is

interesting to note that Dewey's distinction between primary immediate experience and reflective experience or consciousness is
seemingly parallel with Husserl's distinction between the pre-given
world of lived experience or life-world (Lebenswelt as developed
in his *Experience and Judgment*)[28] and the idealizations of science
as objects of reflective consciousness. Husserl's concept of *Lebenswelt* was meant to overcome important objections to subjectivism
as well as to free immediate experience from the garment *(Kleid)*
of ideas thrown by the results of the exact sciences over it. But it
could not achieve either of these aims. His immediate experience
was supposed to be independent of space, objective time and causality; but as Marvin Farber points out:

"The recognition of the pregivenness of nature is only provi-
sional. For the world is accounted for in terms of transcendental
subjectivity, as a construction of experience. Here the distinction
between active experience and passive pregivenness is only pro-
visional; that which was first regarded as pregiven is now viewed
as having its constitutive 'origin' in subjective processes. From the
phenomenological point of view, the origin of the world as a horizon is clarified therewith; and the meaning of the world is traced
to constructive processes in pure experience."[29]

Thus, in Husserl's hands the pregiven world is not the spatial,
temporal world of reality or nature. His 'constitutive' procedure
reduces it to a 'noematic' correlate of 'noetic' experience. Secondly,
Husserl's concept of the 'idealizations of science' proved to be
faulty and inadequate. Here again it will be relevant to quote a
passage from M. Farber:

"The 'idealizations,' and the organized knowledge, are not merely
a garment thrown over some unorganized material. If correct, they
enable us to grasp the nature of the realities in question far more
clearly and extensively than would otherwise be possible."[30]

Dewey's distinction between immediate experience and reflective
experience had a firm naturalistic footing. The 'things' or events of
nature given in direct immediate experience were not merely no-
ematic-correlates of experience. Here primary experience had a
direct 'grasp' of natural being. This grasp was capable of expansion
and sophistication through the instrumentalities of reflective inquiry
in the organized sciences. Organized science was not conceived,

after the manner of Husserl, as casting a veil or garment of ideas over the world. It revealed the depths of nature. Thus, whereas for Husserl all objects are intentional correlates of Transcendental Subjectivity following the 'bracketing' and eventually 'nullification' of the natural world, for Dewey objects of reflective consciousness are the events and things of the natural world with enriched meaning and significance. Husserl's concept of experience led him into the den of subjectivism whereas Dewey's concept of experience as 'transactional' gave experience a firm footing in nature. This is because Dewey fully recognized and realized the significance of the new biology, new psychology and the experimental method of scientific inquiry for a generalized philosophical theory of experience, whereas Husserl failed to grasp this significance and therefore became enmeshed in subjectivistic notions of experience and the well-nigh impossible task of 'constituting' the world out of the subjective depths of the Transcendental Ego. In other words he failed to see the liberating role of a 'methodological pluralism' (in the words of M. Farber) for a genuine philosophy.

In the context of the preceding discussion, it will be easy to understand Dewey's concept of immediate experience. What then are the generic traits of primary experience as revealed by a descriptive-phenomenological procedure adopted by Dewey? What is the 'stuff' or 'structure' of this experience? He conceived all experience in terms of an active interaction between a living organism and a changing environment. The self is not a 'tabula rasa.' If it were it could not survive in a natural environment which is partly hostile and partly friendly. The organism, in its encounter with objects and events, brings to bear upon the environment its entire past experience in the form of habits and attitudes. Experience is the product of this *ongoing transaction*. It is not a passive reception of external sensations. It is not a 'subjective' something occurring 'inside' a mind. It is *constituted by doing and undergoing*. Something is done to the environment and in consequence something is suffered or enjoyed. This interaction consisting of *connections* between "doing-undergoing-doing . . ." constitutes immediate experience for Dewey. He says:

"There are, therefore, common patterns in various experiences, no matter how unlike they are to one another in the details of their subject-matter. There are conditions to be met without which an experience cannot come to be. The outline of the common pattern is set by the fact that every experience is the result of interaction between a live creature and some aspect of the world in which he lives."[31]

Again:

"Experience becomes an affair primarily of doing. The organism does not stand about, Micawber-like, waiting for something to turn up. It does not wait passive and inert for something to impress itself upon it from without. The organism acts in accordance with its own structure, simple or complex, upon its surroundings. As a consequence the changes produced in the environment react upon the organism and its activities. The living creature undergoes, suffers, the consequences of its own behavior. *This close connection between doing and suffering or undergoing forms what we call experience. Disconnected doing and disconnected suffering are neither of them experiences*"[32] (emphasis mine).

Since life's needs are specific and particular we never face 'environment in general.' The notion of *situation* as particular is fundamental to Dewey's theory of experience. A situation is the total context of environmental objects and events *as experienced* by that organism; and it is experienced as *permeated by an immediate and unique quality*.[33] It is the situation which is 'given' existentially. It is a unified whole which includes the psycho-physical organism and specific environmental objects and events. The situation is an active and dynamic field of integrated participation. It is a complex inter-action–moving and dynamic. He says:

"What is intended may be indicated by drawing a distinction between something called a 'situation' and something termed an 'object.' By the term situation in this connection is signified the fact that the subject-matter ultimately referred to in existential propositions is a complex existence that is held together, in spite of its internal complexity, by the fact that it is dominated and characterized throughout by a *single quality*. By 'object' is meant that some element in the complex whole that is defined in abstraction from the whole of which it is a distinction."[34]

Immediate Experience as described above is *qualitative* in three senses. First of all it is an interactional experience characterized by a *unifying pervasive quality*. This pervasive quality is felt as the context or background of our interaction with objects and events. For instance, when we find ourselves in embarrassing, hilarious, distressing or threatening situations our immediate experience is an active 'doing-and-undergoing,' an absorbed participation with various objects of the environment. It is as yet pre-reflective and is held together by a *pervasive quality* which later on (in reflection) may be denoted by the words 'embarrassing,' 'hilarious,' etc. This pervasive quality is a *fused* quality which holds together in a single situation the organism and the objects of the environment with their various 'primary' and 'secondary' qualities. Only when the situation becomes problematic does the organism begin to notice the so-called 'primary' and 'secondary' qualities of the objects in the environment. This original pervasive quality and these 'primary' and 'secondary' qualities are different in kind because the latter are originally fused in the pervasive quality of the total situational experience.[35]

Here then we come to the second sense in which our immediate experience is *qualitative*. We experience the primary and secondary qualities as immediate and belonging to natural objects. They are, like the pervasive quality, qualities of interaction; they belong to objects as *experienced*. Dewey says:

"Interaction of things with the organism eventuate in objects perceived to be colored and sonorous. They also result in qualities that make the object hateful or delightful. All these qualities, taken as directly or enjoyed, are terminal effects of natural interactions. They are individual culminations that give static quality to a network of changes. Thus, 'tertiary' qualities (as they have been happily termed by Santayana), those which, in psychological analysis, we call affectional and emotional, are as much the products of the doings of nature as are color, sound, pressure, perceived size and distance."[36]

By regarding all qualities as the products of the doings of nature, or qualities of interaction Dewey has avoided the 'insoluble puzzles' arising either from regarding them as existing in the 'things' exclusively or in the 'mind' exclusively. The bifurcation of nature is obviated and qualities are restored to where they belong, namely to the objects and things *as experienced*. Anyone who regards this position as unsatisfactory and vague, and continues to demand a specific location for qualities is still suffering from a 'subjective' and 'mentalistic' view of experience and is looking for a spatial image. Unless he is freed from these pernicious assumptions and associations he will not realize the full significance of Dewey's position on quality.

There is a third sense of immediate experience as qualitative. When, as a result of inquiry an indeterminate situation is transformed into a determinate one, it is finally experienced in its *immediacy* with its own *unique, pervasive quality*. This final pervasive quality is richer in content and meaning than the original pervasive quality of the indeterminate situation. This final quality is a consummatory one and, as such, is aesthetic in nature. This is therefore the basic rhythm of experience in Dewey: (i) Immediate qualitative experience of doing and undergoing in specific situations giving rise to (ii) reflective experience in which the organism not only 'has' the experience but understands its meaning or perceives the relation between his 'doing' and 'undergoing.' And (iii) as a result the final phase of experience incorporates the significance and meaning of the reflective phase and is thereby rendered more rich and deepened in its *immediacy*. It is a consummatory experience. In what follows, we shall study how Dewey applies this basic rhythm to his theory of reflective experience eventuating in knowledge, to art and aesthetic experience, as well as to moral experience.

Chapter VI

INQUIRY, KNOWLEDGE AND TRUTH

THOUGH Dewey developed his theory of knowledge in the *Logic* (1938), *Experience and Nature* (1929) and *The Quest for Certainty* (1929) the key to the understanding of his position is provided by an essay on "Qualitative Thought" published in the volume, *Philosophy and Civilization* (1931). As I have pointed out earlier, Dewey wrote this seminal essay under the influence of William James' famous piece, "The Place of Affectional Facts in a World of Pure Experience." I would go further and point out that the key idea elaborated by Dewey in this essay on "Qualitative Thought" provides an understanding of his entire philosophy. Failure to see this point has resulted in some gross misinterpretations of Dewey's position on major philosophical questions. Dewey made a sincere attempt to reply to many unfair and misinformed attacks on his theory of knowledge by B. Russell and A. E. Murphy among others in his "Rejoinder" in the *Schilpp* volume (pp. 517-608). And yet there are certain inherent difficulties involved in Dewey's attempt to 'penetrate' to the 'background' of nature through the 'foreground' of experience. However, in all fairness to Dewey a sympathetic understanding of his position on this question is called for, and will be attempted here.

Dewey believed that the specific philosophical issues, problems and the idiom in which they are posed have to be understood in the context of the larger social, historical and cultural achievements, needs, conflicts and problems. In Dewey's time 'epistemology' or the theory of knowledge together with the problem of the relation of experience to reason was being discussed and disputed interminably within the historically handed down positions of philosophical 'idealism' and 'realism.' First of all, these past theories isolated and eulogised cognitive experience or thought and assigned 'real' character to its objects to the entire exclusion of non-cognitive qualitative experience in which 'things' are 'had' and enjoyed before they are known. Secondly, their theory of experience was outdated, outmoded, and pre-scientific. They adhered to a 'subjectivistic' and 'mentalistic' theory of experience. Dewey points out that most of the traditional dualisms "of the objective and subjective, the real and the apparent, the mental and the physical, scientific objects and qualitied objects, things of experience and things-in-them-selves"–are solved if, as Dewey proposes, the philosophical theory of experience is brought up to date in the light of scientific biology, cultural anthropology and the significance of the experimental method of knowing. Finally, Dewey rightly emphasizes the conti-nuity of experience with nature, and of both with inquiry. Think-ing or rational inquiry is not an alien visitor but it arises within experience through *natural* operations. He therefore invites us in the light of these considerations to 'see' for ourselves what actually takes place in rational and experimental inquiry which eventuates in knowledge. In other words, Dewey is attempting a phenomeno-logical description of the knowing-process–a generalized inquiry into inquiry. Only by such a descriptive account does he hope to rid traditional 'epistemology' of barren and sterile disputes. To begin with, anyone who is sensitive to the knowledge-getting proc-esses in the specialized inquiries of the various sciences will realize that there is no such thing as 'immediate knowledge.' Knowledge is a matter of achievement through the experimentally regulated operations of inquiry. If one understands this, the entire excessive preoccupation of new 'realism' with sterile atomistic 'sense-data' and the absurd idealistic claim of the knowing 'mind' to constitute reality–both must be repudiated. Dewey writes:

"Realistic theories have protested against doctrines that make the knowing mind the source of the thing known. But they have held a doctrine of a partial equation of the real and the known; only they have read the equation from the side of the object instead of the subject. Knowledge must be the grasp or vision of the real as it 'is in itself,' while emotions and affections deal with it as it is affected with an alien element supplied by the feeling and desiring subject. *The postulate of the unique and exclusive relation among experienced things of knowledge and the real is shared by episte-mological idealist and realist*"[1] (emphasis mine).

Here Dewey wants to emphasize that both 'idealism' and 'realism' in their traditional form share a common misconception that knowledge or cognitive experience *alone* has some kind of privileged access to reality or nature. This is because they forget that there is no 'thought' or 'thinking' in general; there is no thought at large. All thought is *contextual* and arises in the context of a problematic situation, and in this situation we experience things and events in their *real* character. Dewey therefore says:

". . . we do not have to go to knowledge to obtain an exclusive hold on reality. The world as we experience it is a real world. But it is not in its primary phases a world that is known, a world that is understood, and is intellectually coherent and secure. Knowing consists of operations that give experienced objects a form in which the relations, upon which the onward course of events depends, are securely experienced. It marks a transitional redirection and rearrangement of the real. It is intermediate and instrumental; it comes between a relatively casual and accidental experience of existence and one relatively settled and defined. The knower is within the world of existence; his knowing, as experimental, marks an interaction of one existence within other existences. There is, however, a most important difference between it and other existential interactions. The difference is not between something going on within nature as part of itself and something else taking place outside it, but is that between a regulated course of changes and an uncontrolled one. *In knowledge, causes become means and effects become consequences, and thereby things have meanings. The known object is an antecedent object as that is intentionally rearranged and redisposed, an eventual object whose value is tested by the reconstruction it effects.* It emerges, as it were, from the fire of experimental thought as a refined metal issues from operations performed on crude material. *It is the same object but the same object with a difference,* as a man who has been through conditions which try the temper of his being comes out the same man and a different man"[2] (emphasis mine).

Again:

"Knowledge attends strictly to its own business; transformation of disturbed and unsettled situations into those more controlled and more significant,"[3] and the "problem of knowledge is the problem of discovery of methods for carrying on this enterprise of redirection."[4]

It is evident from these passages that Dewey intended to put forward an 'instrumental' theory of knowledge which cuts across (i) the 'spectator' theory of knowledge of the new realists where mind is reduced to a passive reflector of a ready made reality, and (ii) the 'idealistic' theory of knowledge which regarded thought as 'constitutive' of reality. Having thoroughly learned from W. James that the organism is an active, interested and dynamic entity, Dewey took a mid-way position which was at once realistic in the truly empirical sense and re-constructive in the sense of conceiving the function of knowing to invest antecedently experienced objects with meaning in the context of experimental inquiry. He therefore brings out this point again in his *Experience and Nature* when he says:

"But idealism, while it has had an intimation of the constructively instrumental office of intelligence, has mistranslated the discovery. Following the old tradition, in its exclusive identification of the object of knowledge with reality, equating truth and Being, it was forced to take the work of thought absolutely and wholesale, instead of relatively and in detail. *That is, it took reconstitution to be constitution; reconstruction to be construction;* . . . a conversion of actual immediate objects into *better,* into more secure and significant objects, was treated as a movement from merely apparent and phenomenal Being to the truly Real. In short, idealism is guilty of neglect that thought and knowledge are histories."[5]

Criticizing the passive character of mind assumed by so-called 'realist' theories of knowledge Dewey continues:

"A realist may deny this particular hypothesis that, existentially, mind designates an instrumental method of directing natural changes. But he cannot do so in virtue of his realism; the question at issue is what the real is. If natural existence is qualitatively individualized or genuinely plural, as well as repetitious, and if things have both temporal quality and recurrence or uniformity, then the more realistic knowledge is, the more fully it will reflect and exemplify these traits. . . . Without the uniformities science would be impossible. But if they alone existed, thought and knowledge would be impossible and meaningless. The incomplete and uncertain gives point and application to ascertainment of regular relations and orders."[6]

It is interesting to note that though Dewey thoroughly assimilated and reflected in his writings the results of the new biology and psychology and grasped the import of the experimental method in the knowledge-process, yet he wrote and talked in the language of 'experience' and followed in his philosophical practice a phenomenological-descriptive method for exploring the nature of knowledge and the nature of Nature. He began with a descriptive analysis of situational or contextual experience, placed the knowing process in the context of the experience of a problematic situation, and pushed back and penetrated into the hinterland of Nature. What saved him from 'subjectivism' was the new biological-anthropological view of experience and the continuity between experience, Nature and inquiry. He writes:

"While, therefore, philosophy has its source not in any special impulse or staked-off section of experience, but in the entire human predicament, this human situation falls wholly within nature. It reflects the traits of nature; it gives indisputable evidence that in nature itself qualities and relations, individualities and uniformities, finalities and efficacies, contingencies and necessities are inexplicably bound together."[7]

What then is inquiry? In one of his celebrated passages in the *Logic* Dewey says:

"Inquiry is the controlled or directed transformation of an indeterminate situation into one that is so determinate in its constituent distinctions and relations as to convert the elements of the original situation into a unified whole."[8]

The appropriate outcome of this inquiry is a judgment 'warrantably assertible' as following validly from the proper use of appropriate methods. Thinking thus arises within an indeterminable situation which has a unique pervasive quality of confusion, doubt or indeterminateness. What is indeterminate about the situation is the *significance* of objects and events in the environment.[9] The indeterminateness of the situation is due to the fact that the on-going process of life does not satisfy a need in the broadest sense of the word (including the need for knowledge for its own sake).[10] The original unique quality of indeterminateness in a particular case controls reflective inquiry until the original situation has been transformed into a determinate one with its own pervasive quality. Without this situational context with its pervasive quality thought would not know where it was going. It would lack unity, control and continuity. All relations of objects in thought are intelligible only as developments and articulations of the initial qualitative situation. Dewey says in his essay on "Qualitative Thought" referred to above:

". . . the selective determination and relation of objects in thought is controlled by reference to a situation–to that which is constituted by a *pervasive and internally integrating quality,* so that failure to acknowledge the situation leaves, in the end, the logical force of objects and their relations inexplicable"[11] (emphasis mine).

Hence, in all thinking the existential subject-matter is a situation with its controlling quality. Since it is *what* is thought about it can only be pointed out in experience. Here Dewey appeals to a direct phenomenological inspection of our experience. He says:

"The situation as such is not and cannot be stated or made explicit. It is taken for granted, 'understood,' or implicit in all its propositional symbolization."[12]

Again:

". . . the situation controls the terms of thought; for they are its distinctions, and applicability to it is the ultimate test of their validity."[13]

The distinction Dewey is making between the existential unified situation and its formulated distinctions and relations of parts has a long historical tradition. That is the distinction between *what* is formulated or talked about and its formulation in discourse, or between the subject-matter and its articulation. Dewey's 'situation' is a substitute for the historical 'substance.' Since 'substance' in its long chequered career accumulated a large number of misleading associations Dewey avoided its use. The 'situation' for him is not a static structure but is a moving, dynamic and functional organization. It is interactional or transactional. Its pervasive quality, therefore, is a moving quality. He says:

"That is, the quality, although dumb, has as a part of its complex quality a movement or transition in some direction. It can, therefore, be intellectually symbolized and converted into an object of thought."[14]

This means that the situation is dynamic; its pervasive quality is a moving quality with a direction. It (the situation) can be inquired into, its details noted and relations of parts articulated.

Dewey attempts to explain this qualitative unity of the situation in psychological terms. He points out that since the situation with its unifying pervasive quality is the existential matrix or the subject-matter inquired into, it cannot be expressed in explicit linguistic formulation. It can only be pointed out in immediate experience. An appeal is made to our experience of such qualitative situations in their immediate existence. This qualitative unity is 'felt' or 'intuited.' Dewey says:

"If we designate this permeating qualitative unity in psychological language we say it is felt rather than thought. Then if we hypostatize it, we call it a feeling. But to term it a feeling is to reverse the actual state of affairs. The existence of unifying qualitativeness in the subject-matter defines the meaning of 'feeling.' "[15]

Again:

" 'feeling' and 'felt' are names for a relation of quality."[16] This amounts to saying that the existential situation with its pervasive quality is prior to its formulation. The universe of experience surrounds the universe of discourse. The pervasive quality of the situation can only be 'felt' or 'intuited.' Recommending the word 'intuition' Dewey says:

"Bergson's contention that intuition precedes conception and goes deeper is correct. Reflection and rational elaboration spring from and make explicit a prior intuition."[17]

"Intuition, in short, signifies the realization of a pervasive quality such that it regulates the determination of relevant distinctions. . . ."[18]

Dewey, however, warns us not to confuse this 'feeling' or 'intuition' with a particular psychological state or a feeling. Pervasive quality of the situation is existentially prior to its later formulation as a feeling in experience. Let us take Dewey's own example to make it clear. Say a person finds himself in a situation whose quality is denoted by the word 'anger.' In such a situation he is in active interaction with objects, things and persons. It is evident that when he *is* angry he is not aware of his feeling or emotion of 'anger' but is actively responding to the persons and objects in their immediate qualities. What demarcates this situation as a unified whole is the pervading quality 'anger.' In later reflection, this person may say that he had undergone an emotion of anger. But now he is entering a new situation whose subject-matter is the prior situation of anger. This new situation of reflective inquiry into a prior situation of anger has its own immediate quality. Now the person is not angry but is examining the prior situation of anger.

It is important to note that, for Dewey, this pervasive quality which demarcates a situation and gives it an internal coherence has a different logical status than the so-called 'primary' and 'secondary' qualities and relations between them. These latter are distinctions of that pervasive quality and are experienced within the context of the unifying pervasive quality. This situational quality is vaguely expressed as the so-called 'tertiary' quality and is affectional in nature. When we say that a situation is 'distressing' we mean to suggest a qualitative wholeness which permeates and colors the objects, things and persons participating in the situation. This unifying quality is not 'subjectivistic' but is a genuine feature of the existential situation in which the organism and the environment participate.

In his essay, "Qualitative Thought," Dewey shows how all reflective thinking arises within a situational context and is controlled by the pervasive quality of that context. This pervasive quality of the situation exercises logical control over all existential propositions formed as a result of reflection over the initial situation. Here he analyzes the Aristotelian treatment of existential propositions and says that though Aristotelian logic recognized the existential nature of qualities, it regarded qualities as static and fixed. It, therefore, gave an attributive or classificatory interpretation of qualities. It took the subject and predicate of an existential proposition as fixed and then it was a problem how the predicate could be attributed to the subject. If the predicate was already contained in the meaning of the subject it was a mere tautology or an analytical proposition; and if it was not, how could it be predicated of the subject? Dewey gives an example: "The red Indian is stoical." He goes on to criticize the traditional analysis of it because it regarded 'red Indian' and 'stoical' as given isolated entities apart from the active reconstructive process of thought. 'Stoicism' was then either attributed as a quality to the Indian as any other quality, say redness, or the Indian was referred to a class of 'stoical persons.' Dewey criticized this analysis as abstract and static; its difficulties arise from its missing the direct 'sense' of the proposition. The direct sense of the above proposition is the situational experience with the pervasive quality stoicism which permeates the entire life and behavior of the red Indian. This is the context which, when discriminated and reflected upon, results in the form of such a proposition. The 'subject' and 'predicate' are distinctions of this pervasive quality of the existential situation and the proposition is the result of active thought which functions within and is controlled by it. He says:

" 'Subject' and 'predicate' are correlative determinations of this quality. The 'copula' stands for the fact that one term is predicated of the other, and is thus a sign of the development of the qualitative whole by means of their distinction."[19]

The 'subject' and 'predicate' are analytic of the 'quality' of the subject-matter, but are additive and synthetic with respect to each other.[20]

Thus reflective and relational thought expressed in propositional forms is guided and controlled by this background of 'pervasive quality' of the existential situation. He gives analysis of some existential propositions in the context of his general theory of pervasive quality of the situational whole in this particular essay.[21] A parallel analysis of similar propositions is given in the *Logic*.[22] It remains to point out that the 'subject' of such existential propositions represents the pervasive quality as means or condition, and the 'predicate' represents *it* as the outcome or end. This is meant to suggest that the situation with its pervasive quality has a structure as well as a function. Reflective analysis brings out the nature of its structure and that of its function. We learn to understand *what* it is (structure) by noting its direction of movement, i.e., by what it does, its end or consequence (function). Not only this, the role of reflective thought is to control, through inquiry, its structure and to use it as *means* for the occurrence of the end. In Dewey's example "The red Indian is stoical" we can say that we know the nature of the 'red Indian' (namely his stoicism) by observing what he does, i.e., the direction of the movement of the total pervasive quality of his behavior in a specific situation. To sum up: Judgment does not attribute a ready-made predicate to a given subject. The function of inquiry is to transform a dubious subject-matter into an articulate existential connection between a subject and an object. The copula of a synthetic judgment stands for existential operations of observations and experiment which invest data with meanings and thus convert them into *objects of knowledge.*

Dewey's theory of knowledge has been misunderstood (i) on the ground of its being *merely* 'instrumental' to a *non-cognitive* experience of enjoying the outcome of knowing in a unified and settled situation, (ii) on its position with respect to the status of 'scientific objects' vis-a-vis macroscopic objects of primary experience and (iii) on its *alleged* denial that antecedent objects are capable of being known.

Dewey has effectively removed all such misconceptions in his "Rejoinder" in the *Schilpp Volume.* He had already anticipated the criticism of the 'instrumental' theory of knowledge when he wrote in *Experience and Nature:*

"It is characteristic of the inevitable moral pre-possession of philosophy, together with the subjective turn of modern thought, that many critics take an 'instrumental' theory of knowledge to signify that the value of knowing is instrumental to the knower. This is a matter which is as it may be in particular cases; but certainly in many cases the pursuit of science is sport, carried on, like other sports, for its own satisfaction. But 'instrumentalism' is a theory not about personal disposition and satisfaction in knowing, but about the proper objects of science, what is 'proper' being defined in terms of physics."[23]

It is because critics have forgotten that Dewey's 'instrumentalism' has to be taken in *two* contexts that they attributed to him the preposterous statement that knowledge is *merely* instrumental to the enrichment of non-cognitive experiences. Dewey says in his reply:

"I had supposed that the contexts within which reference is made, on the one hand to the instrumentality of propositions in the *process* of inquiry to knowledge as warranted solution of a problem, and, on the other, to the instrumentality of *attained* knowledge, through development of intelligence, to enrichment of subsequent experiences, were such as to prevent transferring what is said about one kind of instrumentality to other. . . . There are . . . certain factors common to both kinds of instrumentality. . . . Within the progress of inquiry, for example, intelligent action as the product of previously attained knowledge is constantly taking effect. The termination of inquiry, with respect to the procedures of inquiry that have led up to it, is a resolved situation whose *primary* status and value is cognitional. But the terminal material is also a directly had situation, and hence is capable of treatment on its own account as an enriched experience."[24]

Dewey emphasizes the:

"Function of knowledge-experience as the mode of experience which, through formation of intelligence in action, is the sole instrumentality for regulating the occurrence and distribution of consummatory experiences and for giving them increased depth of meaning."[25] Dewey finally repudiates Russell's 'mischievous' interpretation of his emphasis on 'consequences' as relating to 'personal desire' and 'private satisfaction' when he says:

"The only desire that enters . . . is a desire to resolve as honestly and impartially as possible the problem involved in the situation. *'Satisfaction' is satisfaction of the conditions prescribed by the problem.* Personal satisfaction may enter in as it arises when any job is well done according to the requirements of the job itself; but it does not enter in any way into the determination of validity because, on the contrary, it is conditioned by that determination."[26]

Here it may be relevant to point out that Dewey followed Peirce in his pragmatic conception of truth. It may be relevant to the development of formal deductive systems to hold that propositions are either true or false. But the more important question is: How is *truth* achieved? Truth is not a static, inherent property of propositions. It is the ideal limit of continued inquiry by competent persons. This definition is in keeping with scientific practice. Dewey progressively avoided the use of the word 'truth' because of historical misconceptions and an unending controversy about its nature. Instead he used the phrase 'warranted assertion' in the light of and as a result of competent inquiry. As such 'truth' is fallible; it may be modified in the light of future inquiry. At every stage 'truth' is the outcome of inquiry warranted by evidence.

With respect to the relation between 'scientific objects' and macroscopic objects, Reichenbach has misunderstood Dewey to mean that 'scientific objects' are *merely* relational and therefore somehow 'non-real.' First of all, Dewey agrees with James in his belief in the *existential reality* of relations and connections in experience and nature. He says:

"Long ago I learned from William James that there are immediate experiences of the connections linguistically expressed by conjunctions and prepositions. My doctrinal position is but a generalization of what is involved in this fact."[27]

Moreover, Dewey quotes with approval C. D. Broad as saying that:

"What matters to science is not the inner nature of objects but their mutual relations" (*Scientific Thought*, p. 39). Reichenbach quotes the following passage from Dewey but misconstrues its import because he fails to emphasize the word 'duplicated' in it. The passage is:

"The physical object, as scientifically defined, is not a duplicated real object, but is a statement . . . of relations between sets of changes in other things."[28]

Thus there are no two 'tables'—one qualitative and macroscopic, and the other 'scientific' but there are two different contexts in which the same object is spoken of. He says:

"That the table *as* a perceived table is an object of knowledge in one context as truly as the physical atoms, molecules, etc. are in another situational context and with reference to another *problem* is a position I have given considerable space in developing."[29]

On the third point of criticism of Dewey's theory of knowledge it has been charged by Russell among others that Dewey never tells us about the nature of things before they are inquired into and that he denies that antecedent objects are capable of being known. Rejecting both these charges Dewey points out that as a philosopher he is not supposed to write an "encyclopedia of the conclusions of all sciences,"[30] and that it is the business of specific sciences and inquiries to tell us about the environing world or Nature. He says:

"The business of philosophy, in logic or the theory of knowledge, is not to provide a rival account of the natural environment, but to analyze and report how and to what effect inquiries actually proceed genetically and functionally in their experimental context."[31]

Repeating that objects are events with meaning he says that he has never held "that knowing modifies the object of knowledge. That a planet *as known* is a very different thing from the speck of light that is found in direct experience, I should suppose to be obvious."[32]

Dewey has never denied that antecedent objects are capable of being known. In specific scientific disciplines we may have to inquire into antecedent conditions and objects such as in astronomy and geology. But this knowledge is arrived at the termination of regulated experimental inquiry. Here it should be remembered that the word 'object' is taken in two different contexts—(i) in specialized inquiry and (ii) in epistemological theory.[33] And as to the problem of how from the experienced materials of the present environment we can validly infer the conditions of some past environment one may say that it is to be faced by any theory of knowledge.

Notwithstanding all these clarifications it is time to assess Dewey's attempt to 'penetrate' to the hinterland of Nature through the 'foreground' of experience, and to gauge the final import of his philosophy. Is Dewey's naturalism more predominant or is it his 'experientialism'? No doubt, for Dewey Nature is existentially prior to human existence and experience. But experience, or rather experienced situations are the only 'windows' through which to enter and explore the nature of Nature. Much of the confusion and misgivings in the critics' minds are caused by the fact that in consequence of his Hegelian past, Dewey spoke the language of experience and began by giving a phenomenological description of experience—though, of course, 'experience' was not taken in a 'mentalistic' sense but in interactional sense in the light of new discoveries in biology and psychology. Yet he adhered to the phenomenological method and pushed it to its utmost limits in 'penetrating' and disclosing the nature of Nature. But in this endeavor there are serious limitations.

We ask a question: What is the experiential sign of having attained reliable knowledge at the termination of inquiry? Dewey would say that it is the experience of satisfaction following a settled or reconstructed situation. The whole reconstituted situation is experienced as bathed in a pervasive quality of unification and settlement. But what is the guarantee that this 'satisfactory' experience is not merely a private one but, as Dewey claims, it is conditioned by the objective structure of existence?

Dewey would find it difficult to get back to objective existence if he adhered only to this monistic methodological approach of a phenomenological description of experience and inquiry. This approach is closely akin to James' descriptive approach to the problem of knowledge when he asked: What is its experiential 'cash value'? However, approaching Nature from the side of the experience of 'pervasive quality' may land oneself in a strange predicament reminding us of the famous 'ego-centric' predicament analyzed by R. B. Perry—even when the ego here is a dynamic psycho-physical organism—a live creature, and not the 'pure consciousness' of Descartes or Husserl. No doubt, Dewey asserts in a general way that "experience is *of* nature" and "*in* nature," and emphatically says, "The significance of experience as foreground is that the foreground is of such a nature as to contain material which, when operationally dealt with, provides the clues that guide us straight into Nature's background and into Nature *as* background."[34]

And yet, these statements, though good as far as they go, do not go far enough to break the *circularity* involved in Dewey's position. It may, however, be mentioned to Dewey's credit that he recognized the problem candidly when he said:

"I recognize frankly the circular movement involved, and that the experience which results from interaction with environing conditions contains within itself relations which when followed out tells us about the biological and about the further background—astronomical and geological. In other words, the proof of the fact that *knowledge* of nature, but not nature itself, 'emanates' from immediate experience is simply that this is what has actually happened in the history or development of experience, animal or human on this earth—the only alternative to this conclusion being that in addition to experience as a source and test of beliefs, we possess some miraculous power of intuitive insight into remote stellar galaxies and remote geological eons. In the latter case it is strange that astronomers and geologists have to work so hard to get first certain direct observational experiences and then to get those other experiences by whose aid they interpret and test the evidential value of what is observed."[35]

This is a remarkable admission of the limitation of a purely descriptive experiential approach to nature. Yet the alternative to this approach mentioned by Dewey in the above passage need not necessarily be accepted. Nor the experiential methodological approach be wholly abandoned. Dewey wavered on the verge of seeing but did not actually realize that this 'circularity' could be broken only by the conscious adoption of, what M. Farber[36] has been insisting a 'methodological pluralism' in our approach to Nature. Dewey himself was much wedded to the method of scientific inquiry which involved observation and experiment, and which accepted the results of evolutionary biology, but in his philosophical writings he followed descriptive experiential method alone and forgot to mention that besides this approach to nature one could adopt other methods of inter-subjective verification etc. Certainly, he could not have missed this escape from the self-enclosed experiential approach but for the fact that the logic and the rigor of this phenomenological approach to nature forced him to talk in the language of experience throughout his writings and replies to critics, and not in the language of events.

Our study of Dewey's philosophy of experience and knowledge has brought out at once the value and importance as well as the serious limitations of a purely phenomenological approach to nature through a descriptive analysis of experience and inquiry. And yet Dewey marks a great advance on James. His naturalism is a continuum of potential intelligible structure of nature, experience (which delves into and gets hold of that structure) and inquiry which when experimentally controlled reveals progressively and cumulatively the nature of Nature. This continuum is open-ended —realizing genuinely new possibilities and as such has a temporal and historical character.

Chapter VII

EXISTENCE, EXPERIENCE AND VALUE

D EWEY was basically interested in the great social, moral and
educational issues of his times. He endeavored to bridge the
chasm between knowledge and action, theory and practice by emphasizing *not* that knowledge is merely for the sake of action (as is
commonly misunderstood) but that knowledge itself is an activity
occasioned by a problematic situation. He became involved in the
theoretical controversy about the relation of existence to experience
and of both to value because he recognized that without solving this
issue of theory satisfactorily no effective action could be taken to
tackle the more urgent practical problems facing humanity. And
he found that value-theory was riddled with all kinds of untenable
dualisms handed down by philosophical tradition going back to
the ancient past. He wanted to point out the social and historical
context in which these value-theories developed antedating the
emergence of science as a method of exprimental inquiry. He conceived his task to bring value-theory in line with a new concept of
man in the light of evolutionary biology, dynamic psychology and
the import of the experimental mode of inquiry. Dewey reminds us
that *two* issues have controlled the main course of modern thought:
(i) "Its (philosophy's) central problem is the relation that exists
between the beliefs about the nature of things due to natural science
to beliefs about values–using that word to designate whatever is
taken to have rightful authority in the direction of conduct."[1] Also
(ii) there is ". . . the problem of the relation of physical science to
the things of ordinary experience."[2] We have already dealt with
Dewey's attempt to tackle the second problem mentioned above.
It remains to consider how Dewey approaches the first problem,
namely the relation of existence and experience to value.

Dewey wanted to free ethical theory from the dead weight of
dualisms such as existence (fact) and value, intrinsic and extrinsic

value, objective and subjective value, transcendent and immanent value, and last but not least, means and ends. Here again we find that Dewey employs a descriptive phenomenological method for resolving such theoretical disputes in the light of our 'immediate experience of value-situations. Whenever he finds that thought is entangled in seemingly insoluble and unending paradoxes and perplexities he recommends not merely 'staring' at words and sentences (after the practice of contemporary linguistic analysis) but a direct, immediate inspection of relevant experience. One can discover almost an implicit *epoché* in Dewey's procedure also because he is asking us to free ourselves from all conceptions and assumptions derived from previous intellectual analyses in the light of their cultural contexts. Of course, he did not develop such a phenomenological method to that level of deliberate rigor and perfection as was done by Husserl. Yet, it is unmistakably present in Dewey's approach to the problems of knowledge, value and art. Such an *epoché* with its appeal to direct and immediate experience performs the needed critical function to disengage value-theory from all such untenable dualisms.

He rejects both *intuitionism* and *emotivism* as unsatisfactory theories of value. Both are 'subjectivistic' in import and take ethical issues out of the scope of rational inquiry. The former does so by relying on individual mystical 'intuition' to decide questions of the good and the right; and the latter makes nonsense of moral judgments by declaring that 'good' and 'value' stands for nothing objective but are merely *expressive* of our emotions and attitudes. The force of ethical statements, for them, is *expressive* of our emotions and *persuasive,* and as such they are outside the sphere of rational assessment.[3]

Dewey here applies his key concept of 'pervasive quality' which he elaborated in his essay on "Qualitative Thought" analyzed in the previous chapter. One can discover the basic rhythm of experience (mentioned by me at the end of Chapter V) in Dewey's approach both to moral experience and aesthetic experience.

Exhorting us to go back to immediate experience, Dewey points out that primary experience is not of sense-data but of *situations* which are *transactional.* All thought (in its widest sense) arises within the context of situational experience and is *pervaded* by and bathed in an immediate quality. Though this qualitative wholeness is present in an artistic situation in a heightened and intensified form (as we shall see later), it also characterizes the so-called 'scientific' and 'valuational' thought. Experience, whether it is predominantly 'scientific,' 'artistic,' or 'valuational' is a whole which is 'had' as immediate quality which renders it unique. This pervasive quality demarcates the subject-matter which when inquired into gives rise to explicit judgments. Dewey says:

" 'Scientific' thinking, that expressed in physical science, never gets away from qualitative existence. Directly it always has its own qualitative background; indirectly, it has that of the world in which the ordinary experience of the common man is lived."[4]

This means that scientific thinking which is expressed in propositions has for its point of departure a situation which is problematic in its immediate quality. And this problematic immediate quality, in turn, has for its background the world of primary experience in which the organism and the environment interact in the on-going process of life. Scientific thought arises out of scientific problems, and scientific problems, in their turn, arise out of the needs of the living process. Such a view takes care of both the 'autonomy' as well as the continuity and relevance of science to the process of living.

Dewey traced the alleged dualism between value and existence to the Seventeenth Century Science which left nature bereft of all qualities so that it (nature) appeared, as Whitehead said, ". . . a dull affair, soundless, scentless, colorless; merely the hurrying of material, endlessly meaninglessly."[5]

This had serious implications not only for common sense but for a philosophy of values and qualities—both moral and aesthetic. It gave rise to the 'bifurcation' of nature and to various forms of dualisms. This rigid separation of means from ends, of the *merely* instrumental from the final, of extrinsic value from intrinsic value is, for Dewey, a result of social and historical factors. He says:

"The traditional separation between some things as mere means and others as mere ends is a reflection of the insulated existence of working and leisure classes, of production that is not also consummatory, and consummation that is not productive."[6] He regarded this separation as so damaging both to moral theory and practice that he designated it "the problem of experience."[7] He gave a stirring call for the restoration of means and instrumentalities to their proper level of importance on par with that of ends and finalities. Unless this was done nothing but a total paralysis of effort or a grossly hypocritical allegiance to 'ideals' would ensue. He wrote:

"Means have been regarded as menial, and the useful as servile. Means have been treated as poor relations to be endured, but not inherently welcome. The very meaning of the word 'ideals' is significant of the divorce which has obtained between means and ends. 'Ideals' are thought to be remote and inaccessible of attainment; they are too high and fine to be sullied by realization. They serve vaguely to arouse 'aspiration,' but they do not evoke and direct strivings for embodiment in actual existence. They hover in an indefinite way over the actual scene; they are expiring ghosts of a once significant kingdom of divine reality whose rule penetrated to every detail of life."[8]

Dewey illustrates how the present industrial life gives an index of this rigid separation of means from ends. He says:

". . . economics has been treated as on a lower level than either morals or politics. Yet the life which men, women actually lead, the opportunities open to them, the values they are capable of enjoying, their education, their share in all the things of art and science, are mainly determined by economic conditions. Hence we can hardly expect a moral system which ignores economic conditions to be other than remote and empty."[9]

Again:

"Industrial life is correspondingly brutalized by failure to equate it as the means by which social and cultural values are realized. That the economic life, thus exiled from the pale of higher values, takes revenge by declaring that it is the only social reality, and by means of the doctrine of materialistic determination of institutions and conduct in all fields, denies to deliberate morals and politics any share of causal regulation, is not surprising."[10]

Speaking of how the existential causal connections between

events have to be converted to *meaningful* means–consequence relationship, Dewey says:

"Means are always at least causal conditions; but causal conditions are means only when they possess an added qualification; that, namely, of *being freely used, because of perceived connection with chosen consequences*"[11] (emphasis mine).

Again:

"For all the intelligent activities of men, no matter whether expressed in science, fine arts, or social relationships, have for their task the conversion of causal bonds, relations of succession, into a connection of means-consequence, into meanings."[12] Dewey wanted to bridge the assumed hiatus between science and morals, fact and value, emotion and reflection. He pointed out that scientific objectivity does not mean that the scientist is merely 'mirroring' ready-made 'facts.' It only means freedom from personal bias and prejudice. Valuing is a *fact* of human experience. He urges us to inspect our basic value-experience to find out whether facts and values are irreconcilable or intelligent control of them is possible. He repudiates the claim of the emotivists that evaluative judgments are merely expressive of 'private' emotional attitudes. If that were so, they would render our morals completely chaotic. On the other hand, values cannot be *independent* of our interests and needs. He agrees with R. B. Perry[13] that value in its actual occurrence is the object of any human interest. It is not a transcendental object unrelated to human needs and interests. Things come to possess value-quality in the factual process of being prized and desired. Thus the *experiential locus* of value is the factual situation of prizing things. Both facts and values belong to nature. A concrete value-situation is a *behavioral transaction* in which the situation is experienced as having an immediate quality of being prized, cherished, valued, liked, enjoyed, etc.[14] In its immediate existence this value-quality is what it is. It pervades the whole situation in which the prizing organism and the prized object are included. It is an *existential* subject-matter. But such a value is yet a *candidate*. It is a value *de facto* but not yet a value *de jure*. Only when its claim is questioned with respect to its *conditions* and projected *consequences*, it gives rise to explicit *evaluative* judgments. What was formerly *prized* is now *appraised,* what was valued is now evaluated. This inquiry into its status in terms of conditions and consequences *connects* what we factually value to what we 'ought' to value.[15] It is interesting to note that here Dewey is in essential agreement with what Marvin Farber has to say on the question of value in its twin aspects of actual occurrence and as an outcome of critical, reflective inquiry.

As Marvin Farber says:

"The unit of value or goodness is best defined as the fulfillment of a need or interest, a moral value as the fulfillment of an organization of interests."[16] The phrase 'organization of interests' in this passage corresponds to what comes to be valued as an eventual good as a result of intelligent reflection on conditions and consequences.

There is thus a continuous and cumulative movement of experience between what is immediately valued and what comes out to be valued as a result of critical reflection. Dewey says:

"If intelligent method is lacking, prejudice, the pressure of immediate circumstance, self-interest and class-interest, traditional customs, institutions of accidental historic origin, are *not* lacking, and they tend to take the place of intelligence. Thus we are led to our main proposition: *Judgments about values are judgments about the conditions and the results of experienced objects; judgments about that which should regulate the formation of our desires, affections and enjoyments.* For whatever decides their formation will determine the main course of our conduct, personal and social."[17]

As a consequence of the cumulative experience of problem solving by human beings, certain generalized values come to be adopted as *ends, standards* or *norms.* But these ends are not fixed, ultimate and absolute; they are the projected possibilities of things. They emerge in the factual context of our on-going transactions with nature both physical and social, and do not exist antecedently in a Platonic Heaven. He writes:

"Valuations exist in fact and are capable of empirical observation so that propositions about them are empirically verifiable. What individuals and groups hold dear or prize and the grounds upon which they prize them are capable, in principle, of ascertainment, no matter how great the practical difficulties in the way."[18]

According to Dewey's analysis of value-experience, therefore, what we 'ought' to do is what we 'would' do, if we are rational, in the light of an intelligent appraisal of the conditions and consequences of our actual value-choices. Even the so-called non-rational value-attitudes formed as a result of early social conditioning are, in principle, capable of being inquired into with respect to the conditions in which they were formed and in view of the possible consequences which might follow as a result of persisting in them. Such an inquiry will rob them of their supposed non-rational mystical ultimacy and free the mind from their octopus grip.

From the above account, it is clear that Dewey's approach to the problem of value is in terms of a descriptive analysis of what happens in immediate value-experience as well as in an evaluative-reflective inquiry into it when its status becomes problematic. The limitation of such an exclusive phenomenological approach is its circularity. Ends or Ideals emerge as a result of critical inquiry into our actual value-choices, and at the same time they are used as means or instrumentalities for reorganizing further interests and value-choices. This is the famous Deweyan means-ends continuum. Dewey fought shy of answering the problem of ultimate ends because he feared that when any end was declared to be ultimate it was generally on the basis of unexamined assumptions or class-interests or personal bias. To declare something as ultimate is to take it away from the scope of rational discussion and make it sacrosanct. It was on account of this danger that he did not declare even the happiness of the greatest number of people to be the final end because historically happiness was mistakenly taken to be the 'sum of pleasures' by the Utilitarians. For him happiness was not a static, fixed end but it involved an active process of achieving, fulfilling and realizing one's potentialities. Growing in the sense of continuous reconstruction of experience is the only end which sets free and releases the capacities of human individuals without respect to race, sex, class or economic interests. Dewey writes:

"Nothing but the best, the richest and the fullest experience, is good enough for man."[19]

His faith in the method of intelligent inquiry was so great that he wrote:

". . . that for me the method of intelligent action is precisely such an ultimate value. It is the last, the final or closing, thing we come upon in inquiry into inquiry. But the place it occupies in the *temporal* manifestation of inquiry is what makes it such a value, not some property it possesses in and for itself, in the isolation of non-relatedness. It is ultimate in use and function; it does not claim to be ultimate because of an absolute 'inherent nature' making it sacrosanct, a transcendent object of worship."[20]

Chapter VIII

ART AND AESTHETIC EXPERIENCE

I HAVE been trying to develop in the preceding three chapters that the key concept and guiding thread in Dewey's entire philosophy is that of 'pervasive quality' which he elaborated in that illuminating essay on "Qualitative Thought" which has been referred to more than once already. Now I wish to put forward the thesis that the concept of 'pervasive quality' is the very backbone of his philosophy of art and aesthetic experience. Here again to free the theory of art from preconceived 'metaphysical' or 'subjectivistic' associations Dewey employs and appeals to a phenomenological-descriptive analysis of aesthetic experience and artistic process of creation. In such an analysis he makes use of the basic concepts of "*an* experience" and "consummatory experience,"[1] and makes use of the basic rhythm of experience mentioned earlier.

He points out that various theories of art and aesthetic experience have been propounded. Some of them have been metaphysical, making art esoteric and regarding aesthetic experience as an oblique and symbolic adumbration of a Reality beyond, a glimpse of the splendor of life entirely different from what we know here on earth. Art is said to disclose a realm of 'Being' which has nothing to do with our humdrum world of phenomenal existence. On the other hand, there are theories which make aesthetic experience entirely 'subjective' and 'private'–something occurring inside a 'mind' which is thought of as an alien visitor to this natural world. It has been to the singular merit of Dewey to recognize the futility of all metaphysical, speculative and star-gazing theories of art, and at the same time to retrieve it from thin psychologism. In one of the most stirring and imaginative accounts Dewey has shown the close and intimate relation of art to life. The opening chapters of his *Art as Experience* are an eloquent testimony to it. No exposition can rival what he has said on the subject. It will be our endeavor

103

104 NATURALISTIC PHILOSOPHIES OF EXPERIENCE

to present sympathetically the salient features of his theory of art and point out the influence of "Qualitative Thought" on it.

Dewey thinks that the hiatus between art and life is of recent growth depending on certain historical factors. The museum conception of art which identifies it with the physical art-objects displayed in a museum through the galleries of which people are conducted hurriedly by an official guide, is a peculiar development of modern conditions of complete segregation and compartmentalization of life. When a greater part of modern life is spent in the task of earning and spending, when people's lives are empty of meaning and significance, it is a great compensation for them to pay an occasional visit to an art-gallery or to collect some ancient and antique art-objects to add a pinch of 'culture' to an otherwise drab and colorless life. This, of course, is not meant to deny the aesthetic, educational and cultural functions of museums and art-galleries today, and yet for a vast majority of people art has no direct and intimate connection with life. If one were to study primitive life one would find that this tragic separation of art and life was inconceivable. Dancing, music, painting were a part of the group life concerned with the processes of everyday living. In this rhythm of work and enjoyment, doing and undergoing, people not only lived, but enjoyed an enhanced and heightened sense of living. Dewey says that this "Consummatory" phase—the phase of intensified satisfaction—is the aesthetic phase of our everyday ordinary experience.

"We do not have to travel to the ends of the earth nor return many millenia in time to find people for whom everything that intensifies the sense of immediate living is an object of intense admiration. Bodily scarification, waving feathers, gaudy robes, shining ornaments of gold and silver, of emerald and jade, formed the contents of aesthetic arts, and presumably without the vulgarities of class-exhibitionism that attends their analogue today. . . . Yet in their own time and place, such things were enhancements of the processes of everyday life."[2]

It may be relevant here to point out that though the modern cleavage between art and life is to be deplored, yet it is not without its compensations. No doubt, primitive art was organically related to life. But this very fact hampered its free development. Modern art in its relative independence from the exigencies of life has been able to develop new techniques, new means of expressing the growing experiences of the human race. This is, of course, not to recommend the withdrawal of art into its own 'ivory tower.' It is to emphasize that the synthesis between art and life cannot take place today on the primitive plane of the past. Today the real task of art is neither to withdraw from life and experiences of the people, nor to lose its relative freedom and spontaneity, but to articulate and express through apt media the experiences and values of the people.

Dewey points out that there is nothing mysterious about the intuitive and imaginative nature of artistic experience. It is a well-known phenomenon that artistic experience breaks our habitual, routine and stereotyped ways of 'seeing' things. We break the bonds of dead custom, get out of ruts and experience that freshness of perception which in its quality is truly intuitive and imaginative. Wherever there is a fusion of funded meanings from past experience with a present sense-experience, there is imagination and intuition. The imaginative and intuitive processes in artistic creation appear so suddenly as to seem truly 'revelatory.' It is a rare quality which only a few possess. Imagination is a new way of 'seeing,' feeling and experiencing things. Dewey has, therefore, not tried to explain away some of these psychological aspects of artistic creation and aesthetic experience. He has fully recognized their phenomenological occurrence in experience but has refused to give his assent to any 'spiritual' or 'transcendental' explanation of them. One will notice that throughout his treatment of them he is guided by his fundamental theory of the situational nature of experience with its controlling pervasive quality. Without the control of the existential qualitative nature of artistic experience, it would be difficult to explain all the varieties of psychological experiences in aesthetic perception as well as the aesthetic qualities of the object. Once it is recognized that artistic situation is fundamentally one of cooperation and participation between human energies and other natural energies, it will be seen that artistic quality which pervades the whole situation together with its various discriminations *accrues* to that situation. They are effects or consequences of a thorough participation between the organism and the environment. When this pervasive quality is inquired into in reflective analysis, it is found to reveal the various psychological experiences as well as the various qualities of the work of art. These distinctions are *its* discriminations. Without control by *it* the whole aesthetic situation will fall asunder and it will require many subterfuges to bring them back together. In short, Dewey's theory of art and aesthetic experience is dominated by what we have said earlier about the concept of 'pervasive quality' and that of the basic rhythm of experience.

We shall now analyze Dewey's notions of '*an* experience' and 'consummatory experience' and see how he makes use of these basic notions in discussing aesthetic experience. It is Dewey's general position that there is a continuity between our ordinary experience and other experiences, such as the scientific, moral, aesthetic, and religious. He does not regard aesthetic experience as peculiar or isolated from our ordinary experiences. Patrick Romanell[3] wrongly accused Dewey of confusing art as a special type of experience and as a special phase of it. Dewey's reply[4] to him clarified his position. For Dewey every normal experience has an aesthetic phase, and the so-called 'aesthetic experience' in the arts is only a conscious and deliberate development of that phase of ordinary experience. In two kinds of worlds, there would be no aesthetic experience: a world of mere change or disjointed moments would be a mad-house; a world of no change and movement would be dead, mechanical and lifeless. It is change and order, movement and stability, contingency and regularity that constitute the fabric of life and experience as we know them.

What then is '*an* experience'? Experience gains in quality, intensity, meaning and value as it passes from disequilibrium to equilibrium. The final phase of equilibrium after conflict and resistance is *an* experience which has aesthetic quality. The organism has a tendency not only to be on the move but to tarry, to take a look, and enjoy the harmonius phase of experience. But this has its own dangers in a rapidly moving world, and he who stops too long to 'stand and stare' is in grave danger. The organism has to move, press on and advance, carrying along with it meanings, memories and habits garnered from the past so as to render the present more meaningful and rich and the future full of promise and possibility.

Speaking about '*an* experience' Dewey writes:

"An experience has a unity that gives it its name, *that* meal, *that* storm, *that* rupture of friendship. The existence of this unity is constituted by a *single quality* that pervades the entire experience in spite of the variations of its constituent parts. This unity is neither emotional, practical nor intellectual, for these terms name distinctions that reflection can make within it. In discourse about an experience, we must make use of these adjectives of interpretation"[5] (italics mine).

In order to avoid a possible misinterpretation of Dewey's concept of the consummatory quality of aesthetic experience or of his notion of '*an* experience,' I wish to point out that these concepts have been used by Dewey (though not explicitly) not merely in a descriptive sense but often in a prescriptive sense also. Dewey was an educator, too. He deplored the fact that most of our ordinary experience is either of dull routine or of an aimless drift. In both these cases it is divorced from meaning and significance. In short, it is not *an* experience. Dewey was aware that most of our contemporary art does not possess a consummatory quality, or is *not* expressive of an experience. Contemporary life of anxiety, drift, and meaninglessness is reflected in contemporary art. It would therefore be unfair to accuse Dewey of regarding 'consummatory quality' as *the* common essence of *all* aesthetic experience (creative or appreciative). I therefore maintain that Marshall Cohen, writing on "Aesthetic Essence" in a recently published book,[6] fails to see this point. He points out that "consummatory quality is more frequently associated with sexual than with artistic experience, and various artistic techniques . . . are often exploited to create just that gappy 'breathless,' or discontinuous quality that Dewey assigns to practical experience" (119).

Here, again, Dewey's concept of pervasive quality would throw light on the nature of *an* experience. Every experience in its situational context has a dynamic, moving, pervasive quality that is immediately felt. It is a whole of parts which move through conflict and resistance. As the pervasive quality moves through tension, the organism becomes conscious of the process, perceives the relation between discriminated qualities *within* the initial pervasive quality till the process reaches consummation. The final situation thus reached has its own pervasive quality which has been enriched by the consciousness of the process. Dewey's point is that this moving quality makes an experience *an* experience in so far as it involves the thorough incorporation of the process with the final end, of the means with the consequence. Only when the relation of means (process) to the final phase of consequence is *perceived* is the whole experience meaningful, significant and valuable. It is *an* experience. This interpenetration of means and ends constitutes for Dewey an artistic experience having the final aesthetic phase.[7]

As I have pointed out above, Dewey has mixed descriptive and prescriptive elements in his account of '*an* experience' and 'consummatory experience.' This has given rise to misinterpretations of Dewey's theory of art. If Dewey had said that *all* ordinary experience and *all* aesthetic experience *actually had* this *common* quality, his position would be untenable. This thorough incorporation of means and ends, instrumentality and finality is not actually present in all ordinary experience or in all aesthetic experience. What Dewey implies is that in *genuine* art it does take place and that it *can* be there in our daily experiences. He was not so naive as to fail to notice that most of our experience is either routine or disjointed. In both cases it is sundered from meaning. Such routine and disjointed experiences are not experiences in the most significant and pregnant sense of 'experience.' Such a separation of means and ends in our experience is due to special causes which lie in our cultural conditions; therefore it need not occur, in the nature of the case.

Does Dewey imply that we can recapture even today the primitive harmony between art and life? In other words, do we discover a moral 'ought' in his conception of *an* experience? It is his faith that this 'ought' implies a 'can' and that every experience has a potentiality of becoming an organic whole. He implies that to be fully alive, to be human, we should so plan our lives and activities that they are neither mechanical and meaningless drudgery nor a hedonistic abandon to passing impressions. How far this is possible for all of us in contemporary times is a question not for aesthetics but for sociology, politics, education, and above all for individual initiative. Dewey therefore has not always kept the descriptive and normative accounts of aesthetic experience apart and has, consequently given rise to some misunderstandings as mentioned above.

A comment on Marshall Cohen's point (op. cit.) that consummatory quality is associated more with sexual experience than with aesthetic experience, will not be out of place here. Cohen forgets that Dewey emphasized a continuity between our ordinary experiences and aesthetic experience in the arts. I have shown above that every experience can have an aesthetic phase. Art, for Dewey, is a quality that permeates experience. He rejects the "ivory tower" view of art. Hence sex experience also *can* be either a mechanical affair (as sexual promiscuity proves) or it *can* have a genuine consummatory quality–an aesthetic quality–if it occurs within the context of a genuine experience in which the total personalities of the participants are involved in mutual love and respect. In other words, only when sex experience does not function in isolation but is incorporated in the total and complex fused quality of love, is it entitled to be called aesthetic or genuinely consummatory. Jules Romain's novel *The Body's Rapture* is an eloquent testimony to what Dewey has in mind.

In *Art as Experience* Dewey develops this thesis with consummate skill. The artistic 'idea' (not to be confused with the Lockean or Humean 'idea') is the total initial quality of the experience with which the artist starts. It is only a vague something in the beginning. It is a dumb quality. It is 'felt' in its immediacy as the initial subject matter. Since it is a dynamic idea or quality, it moves, and the artist begins to work it out or express it progressively through a medium, whether in colors, lines, volumes, masses, sounds, or words. The artist does not know the outcome as he proceeds and manipulates his materials. But the process is not blind. At each stage of development there is a perception of relations between what the artist has done and what he is going to do. In other words, doing and undergoing, activity and enjoyment of meanings go side by side in the artistic process. The whole process is controlled and guided by the initial pervasive quality–supplemented, modified, and developed by the perception of qualities of the intermediate stages. Creative artists like Picasso[8] and Henry James (to take two illustrations only) confirm Dewey's view on the role of pervasive individualizing quality in the creative process. Henry James' own "Preface to the Spoils of Poynton"[9] is a good discussion of the actual creative process at work. Speaking of how he got the 'germ' of his story from one of the allusions made by a lady during the course of a talk, he writes:

"The germ, wherever gathered, has ever been for me the germ of a 'story' and most of the stories straining to shape under my hand have sprung from a single small seed, a seed as minute and wind-blown as that casual hint for the 'Spoils of Poynton' dropped unwittingly by my neighbor, a mere floating particle in the stream of talk. . . . Such is the interesting truth about the stray suggestion, the wandering word, the vague echo, at touch of which the novelist's imagination winces at the prick of some sharp point: its virtue is all in its needle-like quality, the power to penetrate as finely as possible" (147).

The essential artistic criterion for Dewey is a heightened, intensified, and deepened experience of the qualities of things and events. This intensification in art, as in life, takes place through conflict and resistance. What would life be if we were to roam about in a world of abstract mathematical formulas and mere intellectual relations? We would miss the 'feel' of life, the 'tang' of quality that makes life precious, worthwhile, and meaningful. Anyone who has undergone *an* experience of love, tragic disappointment, or intimate friendship has felt life in its immediate quality and poignancy. Dewey has underscored the role of conflict within the integrating and unifying pervasive quality as that of clarifying, intensifying, and heightening the qualitative feel of things, events and processes. He writes:

"That which distinguishes an experience as aesthetic is conversion of resistance and tensions, of excitations that in themselves are temptations to diversion, into a movement toward an inclusive and fulfilling close (Art as Experience, 56)."

The above analysis of Dewey's philosophy has shown that the concept of 'pervasive quality' dominates it throughout and that it is the quintessence of his philosophy of art and aesthetic experience. An adequate analysis and understanding of Dewey's concepts of 'an experience' and 'consummatory experience' require a prior grasp of this notion of 'pervasive quality.' Without the control of this individualizing quality, the whole aesthetic situation will fall apart and render aesthetic experience unintelligible. And yet we have seen that his concept of 'an experience' blends in an imperceptible manner descriptive and normative elements, giving rise to misinterpretations of his theory of art. Once again sheer description has been found to have its own limitations.

Section C

MARVIN FARBER

Chapter IX

MARVIN FARBER AND THE PROGRAM OF NATURALISTIC PHENOMENOLOGY

R EACTING to ideas and perspectives derived early in his career from Marx and the evolutionists, Marvin Farber belongs to that distinguished tradition in American philosophy to the shaping of which Dewey devoted a lifetime in the not too distant past. Notwithstanding his legitimate criticism of some aspects of Dewey's philosophy he, like Dewey, has seen the philosophic enterprise in the total context and perspective of social and historical factors against the backdrop of nature.[1] Having studied with Edmund Husserl, the founder of 'pure' phenomenology, in the latter's Freiburg period, Farber has performed an important historical function of not only interpreting Husserl's philosophy in its developing phases and bringing it to the American shores, but also pointing out with clarity, vigor and characteristic boldness the limitations of phenomenology when viewed in the light of the comprehensive aims of general philosophy. *The Foundation of Phenomenology* first published in 1943 and now in its third edition (State University of New York Press, 1967) remains a source book, and is one of Farber's major contributions to a critical understanding of Husserl's *Logische Untersuchungen*. During his philosophical career, spanning over a period of four decades, commencing in an important sense with his *Phenomenology as a Method and as a Philosophical Discipline* (University of Buffalo Publications in Philosophy, 1928) he has maintained a continuity of outlook in viewing phenomenology as one of the important methods of philosophizing but at the same time pointing out that when adopted as an exclusive method it has led to perverse subjectivism. He has regarded phenomenology as the last stronghold of anti-naturalistic philosophy of subjectivism and idealism. Instead of throwing out

115

the baby with the bathwater and repudiating phenomenology altogether, he has been developing throughout these years the theme
of a 'naturalistic phenomenology' based on the concepts of 'ontological monism, and logical and methodological pluralism.' His
Naturalism and Subjectivism and the recent Harper and Row
Torchbooks publications[2] have continuously pointed towards that
goal. And in one of his most recent papers[3] he has used the phrase
"the program of a naturalistic phenomenology," and explored and
developed the outline of such an enterprise. It will be our aim to
explicate and to evaluate Farber's concept of 'naturalistic phenomenology.'

Could there be such a thing as 'naturalistic phenomenology'?
Orthodox followers of Husserl as well as those who have taken
the various forms of 'existentialism' seriously might react strongly
against the very possibility of such a program, and even regard
it as preposterous. Is it not the case that a thoroughgoing
naturalist like Farber, in conceiving of an alliance between phenomenology and naturalism, is still evincing a strong continuing
influence–subtle and subterranean–of "one of the honored masters
of his youth"? Scholars outside of the phenomenological tendency
might wonder as to the reasons why Farber has not been able to
throw off the 'uncanny spell' cast by Husserl on his mind and
thought. Professor B. E. Bykovsky–a Russian scholar–has gone to
the extent of saying that though Farber is "trying to avoid the reac-
tionary consequences of phenomenology," yet his thought represents an attempt to "cultivate phenomenology without raising its
fruits."[4] A careful reading of Farber's works will show that unlike
many uncritical admirers of phenomenology, he has endeavoured
to bring out both the importance as well as the limitations of phenomenology. He has reacted strongly against the subjectivistic program of Husserl's later 'transcendental and constitutive' phenomenology. He has been unsparing in his criticism of 'existentialism'
in its diverse forms by branding them as 'irrational off-shoots' of
classical Husserlian phenomenology. They have been seen as having
inherited the subjectivistic thesis of the primacy of the human experiencer combined with a non-rationalistic concept of experience.
Husserl had, at least, maintained throughout a thoroughgoing
rationalistic concept of philosophy as a 'rigorous science.' 'Philo-

sophical anthropology' as envisaged by Max Scheler and the 'existentialisms' of Heidegger and Sartre have, in Farber's view, opened the floodgates of irrationalism. Their attempt to understand the world through the so-called 'primary structures' or universal human *existentialia* of care *(Sorge)*, anxiety *(Angst)*, being-unto-death *(Sein-zum-Tode)*, estrangement *(Entfremdung)*, guilt *(Schuld)* and resolve *(Entschlossenheit)* in the case of Heidegger, and those of 'naughting' *(néantisation)*, 'radical freedom' and 'nausea' in the case of Sartre, have proved abortive in their pretended presumptuousness. These dramatically selected emotional moods and traits of human experience have been isolated, mystified and absolutized for effect, and declared, *ex cathedra*, as significant ontological categories. Farber has pricked the pomposity of such self-styled profundities.[5] Nor does Farber see eye-to-eye with some uncritical attempts at 'phenomenologizing' at certain American Universities because of their failure to see the subjectivistic implications of such a procedure.

In order to assess Farber's concept and program of naturalistic phenomenology it will be advisable to begin with the aims and functions of philosophy as viewed by Husserl through the various phases of his phenomenology. What are, after all the aims of philosophy? What is philosophy about? Where do we begin? What is the 'given' for philosophical reflection? It is easier to raise such questions than to answer them. There is such a bewildering disagreement among practising philosophers today about the *meaning,* aim and function of the philosophical enterprise that it will be hazardous to give any simple, dogmatic answer to these questions. Is it advisable to limit the scope of philosophizing to a 'perpetual sharpening of the tools' in the form of *mere* linguistic or conceptual analysis after the fashion of ordinary-language philosophers? Or again, should philosophy be identified with a phenomenological 'clarification' of all concepts in terms of the consciousness of an individual knower? However useful these attempts may be in their limited perspective both these approaches share a common weakness of 'detaching' the philosopher from his social and historical context. They are philosophies of 'withdrawal' and 'resignation' trying to justify their standpoint on the dubious separation of the philosopher *qua* philosopher from the philosopher *as* man. Probably they reflect the troubled and uncertain times in which we live and are a sign of the philosopher's unwillingness to "rub his shoulders and hurt his elbows" in the rough-and-tumble of difficult and often distressing social and political problems of the contemporary world. It is heartening to find that Farber, and there he is in agreement with Dewey, is highly critical of such an 'ivory tower' concept of philosophy, and the narrow and limited role of philosophers as solving or 'dissolving' philosophical puzzles which they themselves have helped to create. In other words, as Dewey would say, contemporary philosophers have developed a rigid 'in-group' attitude, and as such, they address their papers of technical analysis to the alleged solving of one another's problems rather than to the substantive issues and 'problems of men.' No wonder the world of concrete social and historical realities passes them by. Farber warns us against such an artificially created atmosphere of aloofness and academic irresponsibility when he says:

"If philosophy is to bring wisdom to others, it must not be misled by narrow and unclarified motives, nor warped by irrationalism and verbal jugglery, which at times seems indistinguishable from downright lunacy."[6]

He reminds the philosophers "of the time-honored functions of philosophy: clarification of basic ideas, periodical synthesis of the chief results of the sciences, methodology, and the continued elaboration of a theory of values."[7]

Equipped with such a comprehensive and imaginative concept of the role of philosophy, Farber has reacted critically to the aims and functions of Husserl's phenomenology. Husserl was motivated by the quest for *certainty* and *absoluteness* of knowledge. His search was directed toward an absolutely *presuppositionless* beginning. He did not find such 'givenness' either in the natural-inductive sciences or in the deductive-mathematical sciences because, according to him, all of these disciplines *assumed* some *concepts* which were left unclarified. He was inspired by the grandiose rationalistic program of founding philosophical knowledge in an absolutely certain and indubitable *insight*. His *Ideas* and his *Cartesian Meditations* were attempts to radicalize Descartes' dream of an absolute beginning. He hit upon the concept of phenomenological 'seeing' or 'insight' into the essential structures of experience. Conceiving

PROGRAM OF NATURALISTIC PHENOMENOLOGY

philosophy as a rigorous science, Husserl performed the now famous *epoché*–putting the whole of natural knowledge in 'brackets'
and making no assumptions about anything whatsoever. With his
call "Back to the things themselves" he sought the ultimate foundations of all our rational knowledge in an immediate vision–the
original data of our consciousness. His guiding rule was that whatever manifests itself 'originarily' in its 'primordial' 'self-givenness' or
'bodily presence' to our consciousness is apodictically evident, true
and certain. It needs no other foundation. With the master-stroke
of a genius Husserl put forward the phenomenological method of
suspending all judgments, shedding all bias and prejudice, putting
in abeyance our habitual modes of perceiving things, and thus
learning to 'see' things in an original and radical way. Phenomenological reflection was thus a call for a radical change in attitude (it
should not be confused with psychological introspection)–a me-
thodic procedure to penetrate deeper and deeper into things and
unravel 'layers' beneath what we habitually saw or thought. To
arrive at such a rock-bottom foundation of our knowledge he made
use of the eidetic reduction and the various phases of the 'phenomenological reduction.' Eidetic reduction was meant to 'reduce' the
world of *facts* to the world of general a-priori *essences,* because
facts were contingent, and therefore could not be used as an absolute foundation. This reduction opened for him the entire field of
noetic-noematic structures of experience for analysis such as perceiving, remembering, imagining, judging, believing, etc., etc. With
the help of memory, modifications in perception and 'free-variation'
in phantasy he sought to arrive at those immutable and invariant
essences of things which could not be changed without changing
the *nature* of the things under study. These identical 'pre-constituted'
essences were, however, to be seized in an active grasp of intuition.
Apart from the eidetic reduction there was to be the strictly phenomenological reduction by which the whole 'world of being' was
put within 'brackets' together with our cultural-scientific world
which was reduced to the *Lebenswelt* or the world of our immediate experience. Farber has rightly recognized Husserl's originality
and genius in not only conceiving such a rationalistic descriptive
method of phenomenological analysis in a programmatic manner,
but also in the many fruitful and illuminating analyses he offered

in the field of logic and mathematics which he presented in his famous trilogy of *Logische Untersuchungen, Formale und Transzendentale Logik* and *Erfahrung und Urteil*.[8] Such an appreciation has, however, not prevented Farber from strongly criticizing Husserl's shift to subjectivism and idealism via the latter's concept of the *intentionality* of consciousness and the *transcendental reduction* which leads us from the phenomenologically reduced world of objects and the worldly 'I' to the transcendental Ego or Subjectivity. In his later 'constitutive phenomenology' Husserl almost forgot that his phenomenological reduction was merely a methodological procedure for radical reflection, and that his definition of consciousness in terms of its intentionality or directedness to a 'meant' object was suited only for a descriptive analysis of the noetic-noematic structures of experience. No doubt for such descriptive purposes 'real' historical objects could be 'suspended' but no illicit use of such a definition of intentionality could be made for denying the ontological independence of those objects. As conceived by Husserl the 'object' appears as essentially determined by the structure of consciousness and his treatment of 'transcendence' deals not with the reality of the historical object but with the essential meaning of the object. Consequently intentional analyses become 'constitutive analyses' meant to describe and explain how the meaning of things is primordially constituted in and through consciousness.

Recognizing the merits of some of Husserl's admirable analyses of, say, time-consciousness, the act of perception in which the perceived object is given *perspectively* with its 'internal' horizon and 'external' horizon, and of the origin of logical forms and concepts in experience, Farber has, however, pointed out practically in all his major works that no metaphysical use could legitimately be made of such analyses. But as a matter of fact, in his transcendental phenomenology, Husserl not only 'bracketed the world' but almost 'nullified' it, and conceived its program as that of 'constituting' not only the *meaning* of the world but also the *existence* of the world. The fatal idealistic slip was made and existence was declared to be dependent on the knowing mind. Even the *Lebenswelt* of immediate experience was to be 'constituted' in and by transcendental Subjectivity. It is evident that Husserl's alleged 'radical' beginning was not so radical after all. The actual historical world of existence and the existence of other Egos became a *problem* for Husserl's 'constitutive phenomenology.' He failed to see that these were purely, in Farber's words, 'methodogenic' problems. In his excessive preoccupation with essences and absoluteness Husserl ignored the *basic* fact that the knowing subject is not a 'bloodless' transcendental spectatorial Ego, but a living historical person conditioned by nature, evolution and cultural traditions. Farber writes:

"The phenomenologist proposes to reflect with the greatest possible thoroughness, and to question his experience about the evidence for other persons, so that he feels compelled to begin as an individual. Unless he is careful to acknowledge clearly the factual and *real* priority of nature and society to the individual, he is apt to become involved in archaic nonsense, no different from the speculative excesses so prominent in the tradition of philosophy."[9]

Again:

"The process of reflection must be extended to include a view of the thinker in his historical conditions. There must not only be an *epoché* with regard to concepts and principles; the thinker must be viewed in his position in society and in cultural history. What are his interests? How do they bear upon the questions at issue? He may indeed, and with right, be led by his interests. So long as he does so explicitly and announces that fact, he is not guilty of the usually covert error of being influenced by his interests while claiming personal detachment and social 'neutrality.' It is necessary to reduce all normative statements, all preferences, to theoretical propositions, so that they can be tested. The philosopher who has no preferences, no interests of any kind, is a fiction."[10]

Farber, in the interest of truth, does not shrink from almost a 'frontal' attack on Husserl when he says that:

"Husserl never freed himself from all antecedent, philosophical commitments, despite his claims of neutrality and evidence."[11]

Again:

"While radical in his way, Husserl was himself naive with respect to human society and history. He knew very little about the positive findings of social scientists and objectivistic philosophers, and he was really not very much interested in socio-economic problems. He was interested in a non-temporal ('supertemporal') order which he extolled as being above the lowly mundane order of problems.

Even his treatment of intellectual history in one of his most mature writings was detached from the realities of history."[12]

After all, can one really *begin* philosophizing with an absolutely clean slate without any presuppositions? One can, of course, become aware of one's assumptions and avoid getting involved in ordinary fallacies and alleged 'insoluble' entanglements. Husserl himself was a very sophisticated thinker–rooted in his times and reacting to what he conceived to be the dogmatic naturalism and psychologistic tendencies of the period. It is another matter that his understanding of naturalism turned out to be a bit naive. It requires a very sophisticated outlook–a trained reflective mind–to make a 'presuppositionless' beginning. In strictness, for Farber as for Dewey before him, all beginnings in philosophizing are *contextual*, and as such, are rooted in specific problems, whether they are epistemological, logical, scientific, moral or social. Sheer description is merely an ideal. Farber does not deny the importance and legitimate place for what he correctly calls 'cross-sectional' phenomenological analysis, especially in the field of formal logic and mathematics. But that does not mean that any ontological conclusions in favor of idealism and subjectivism can be drawn from such an analysis. Of course, the concept of being or existence too can be 'clarified' through phenomenological analysis in terms of direct experience of an individual thinker. But, as Farber points out:

"If one is not to incur the use of a dogma that may be called 'determination by initial clarification,' declaring the clarified being to be the only possible being, one must return to actual facts. That is to say, to our knowledge of being, of existence, of the world, and of man and his activities, as provided by our common experience, direct and culturally inherited, and by the sciences."[13]

Moreover, is not this pursuit of *certainty* in knowledge a bit too morbid? May it not masquerade a desire to 'safeguard one's vested interests'? In most practical problems of empirical nature, one has to be satisfied with adequate practical verification. In formal disciplines, one may not violate the law of contradiction. But the attempt to found all knowledge whether formal-mathematical or natural-empirical in an indubitable intuition of essences 'constituted' in pure consciousness, is too ambitious and presumptuous.

One does commit errors in the description of these so-called essential structures as in the case of naturalistic descriptions. All these descriptions are subject to the demands of inter-subjective comparison and verification, and no one, including Husserl, can be credited with the *final* authority in such matters. If one insists on such an indubitable certainty, one will be condemned to what Farber calls a "solipsism of the immediate moment" and that too at the moment of its occurrence. Often, as in the analysis of the perception of a thing in terms of 'perspectival shadings,' what is declared to be on the basis of a priori 'eidetic insight' can be equally arrived at on the basis of *factual* knowledge. What is gained by all this talk about 'eidetic insight' except a dubious claim to self-styled 'seeing' with certainty and absoluteness?[14]

Commenting upon such analyses of the perceptual situation Farber says:

"The formulation of this fact in terms of essences is merely a way of borrowing empirical facts and outfitting them as 'essential necessities' expressing 'rules.' "[15]

Farber raises the very pertinent issue of the value and usefulness of 'intentional analyses' and phenomenological 'clarification' of concepts, especially in the field of social and moral inquiry. Do we gain in 'clarification' (if so, of what sort) when we say with Husserl that the valuing consciousness constitutes a new kind of 'axiological' objectivity giving rise to a new regional ontology? Is it not a bit too trifling to say that we become aware of value in valuing consciousness? Do not our actual social and moral problems merit a better treatment of value than is offered in 'intentional analysis'? Much has been made of the 'tremendously' important discovery that consciousness is essentially intentional in the sense of being directed to a *meant* object. Without totally disparaging a phenomenological description of values Farber, however, points out that:

"The major value problems of our time may be stated, understood, and possibly solved, without waiting for the phenomenological clarifications. It will be sufficient at this time to mention such problems as capital and labor, war and peace, and the individual and society. It would be a sad thing, if agreement among philosophers on 'timeless' fundamentals were prerequisite to the solution of the great problems of mankind. The world might well go to ruin before even an appreciable minority got to the second underpass in the 'reduction.' "[16]

It will be apparent from what has been said above that Farber is highly critical of Husserl's transcendental phenomenology because of its idealistic and subjectivistic implications. He is prepared to give due place to conceptual clarifications at a reflective level. And here descriptive phenomenology is welcome as *one* of the methods for dealing with specific types of problems. But no metaphysical or ontological conclusions can be allowed to be drawn from such a descriptive procedure. 'Clarified' concepts and meanings are always fruitful in all inquiries—both natural and phenomenological. Farber will go along with such 'clarifications' provided they are recognized to have their place in the context of nature. No talk of 'transcending' nature is to be brooked if philosophers are to avoid making a laughing-stock of themselves. To say that all objects are experienced and therefore their *existence* depends on our experiencing is to repeat a childish argument. Subjectivism cannot toy with the statement that one never gets beyond experience. Farber says:

"It is unavoidably true, but trivial, that experience indicates and presupposes the presence of experience. There are no ontological consequences of that statement. On the other hand, it can be said that as a matter of fact one never gets beyond nature. But one can think 'beyond' nature, in the sense that ideal entities and possibilities can be entertained or utilized. That does not mean transcending nature. Even the capacity to entertain ideal entities in thought, and the occasion for devising them, may be traced out to real social-historical conditions."[17]

Farber's pervasive naturalism is meant to restore healthy-mindedness and bring in 'fresh-air' to the stuffy atmosphere of the highly-strung and the 'tremendously serious' posture of transcendental phenomenology. It is time to have a look at what he means by 'nature' and the way he conceives man's place in it. Though Farber sometimes uses 'naturalism' and 'materialism' interchangeably to describe his position it will be a mistake to interpret him to mean by these terms any narrow mechanistic view of nature. He places man and his experience within nature and relies on the cumulative and the progressively correctible methods and findings

of the natural and social sciences. His concept of nature is a comprehensive, imaginative and open-textured picture which emerges
as a generalized result of the findings of special sciences. It may be
proper to regard him as a 'critical' naturalist or materialist without
incurring any of the opprobrium attached to the latter designation.[18]
Because of recent interest in existence and especially in human
existence in the writings of those who are grouped under 'philosophical anthropology' and various types of 'existentialism,' Farber
has devoted a good deal of attention to the general problem of
existence and a critical evaluation of the 'pompous' philosophies of
Heidegger, Sartre, Osker Becker and Jaspers. Farber's treatment of
human existence and its place in natural existence is also immensely
useful in evaluating the recent proliferation of what is called 'philosophical psychology' within the movement of ordinary-language
philosophers. The assumption common to both 'philosophical anthropology' (including 'existentialism') and 'philosophical psychology' is to treat mind and human existence as completely *sui generis*
–to the understanding of which causal-genetic analysis is declared
to be totally irrelevant. A sharp distinction is made between reasons and causes, values and facts, normative commitments and
causal conditions. An impression is sought to be created according
to which man is conceived to belong altogether to an independent
and autonomous realm of being–which can be disclosed through
either an esoteric 'existential' analysis of *Dasein* or through a verbal
report of reasons which a particular man gives for his behavior.
No critical student of philosophy will disagree with the following
evaluation of the existentialistic mode of philosophizing made by
Farber after careful study:

"The subjectivistic limitations of phenomenology brought on
efforts to correct them within the fold of the idealistic and fideistic
traditions. Existence had to be dealt with, or at least the word
existence had to be brought to the forefront of interest. The ex-
travagant claim has been made that the problems of existence and
of being were at least lost sight of until recent existentialists called
attention to them. Heidegger has been given credit for deepening
the understanding of these problems, despite the unusual amount
of plodding necessary to extract meanings from a frequently opaque
text. The results are largely disappointing and unsatisfactory. Banal

platitudes are dressed up to serve as profundities; sweeping general-
izations (such as care as a fundamental feature of existence, and
the role of the idea of death) are foisted upon the reader as absolute verities, with no attempt at critical justification; and linguistic
turns, whether subtle or outrageous, are trumpeted as philosophical
advances. The persistent fog and the awkward difficulty of the text
seem to have the function of protecting the small amount of
thought and magnifying its importance."[19]

There is, therefore, no sense in speaking of a general problem of
'human existence.' There are concrete, specific and particular problems such as social, political, personal, economic and moral—which
man faces in the ongoing course of transaction with natural and
cultural events. There is no evidence to believe that the human
mind is 'above' or 'beyond' nature. There is no short-cut to the
understanding of the human mind and existence through 'mystical'
and 'profound' pronouncements or through verbal reports of 'trans-
parent reasons' given by individuals for their behavior. The whole
mode of such an approach is too deceptive and simplistic. Farber
rightly points out that the "understanding of the human mind depends upon physical, physiological, and psychological facts; but
also upon social and cultural facts. It is added to by the structural
findings of 'pure' phenomenological inquiry."[20] Farber is not assimi-
lating the human mind and behavior to a single mechanistic type of
explanation. Though human behavior is conditioned by physiological and physical factors, it also reveals 'emergent' qualities due to
the complex organization of the human brain and the social-
historical nature of the cultural environment with which man is in
continuing and cumulative transaction. Farber contends cogently
that a sound and reliable ontology can be constructed on the basis
of the principle of 'ontological monism' combined with 'methodological and logical pluralism.' Such a position can take care of the
diversity of the facts involved without giving up the basic unity of
'natural and physical events.' He says:

"The nature and organization of the basic physical units account
for the different types of properties and behavior in the inorganic,
organic and cultural realms. This view leaves out nothing that can
be descriptively established. Even the most abstract activities of the
'pure' reflective (or 'transcendental-subjectivistic') investigator may

be fully allowed for on this monistic basis. Man is not debased thereby. On the contrary, he feels a greater sense of dignity, earned by the understanding that progress through science in all its forms –natural and formal, empirical and abstract–may eventually enable him to solve all important problems. Therein lies the optimistic outlook of this balanced and logically weighted naturalism."[21]

'Methodological pluralism' implies that no single method is suitable for solving all kinds of problems. Methods are to be judged on the basis of their suitability and relevance for solving specific types of problems. Thus a place is found for 'cross-sectional' subjectivistic method of descriptive analysis (conceptual and formal) as well as for 'longitudinal' (historical and evolutionary) method depending upon the type of problem encountered. Farber scouts all attempts at 'phenomenologizing'–seeking to give a 'phenomenological foundation' to our natural and social sciences–as misguided and overly ambitious. Such a "rationalistic ideal of a single tree of knowledge, with all the sciences branching out from the one trunk, underlying which are a few 'root ideas,' "[22] is a utopian pomposity. Of course, concrete problems encountered in the natural sciences between 'experienced qualitative objects' and 'scientific objects' (electrons, genes, ions, etc.) can be handled through the scientific determination of evidence in competent inquiry without falling into a subjectivistic trap. Once it is recognized that inquiry itself is a complex event and "all inquiry is within nature, with multiple conditioning factors"[22a] within a social and cultural tradition, no subjectivistic conclusions need follow. Moreover one should never forget that the "causal conditions of experience are physical, organic and cultural,"[22b] and as such its locus is in nature.

Farber's principle of 'logical pluralism' recognizes that different systems of knowledge can be validly constructed in the natural, social and formal sciences on the basis of the principle of the 'cooperation of methods.' In the social and the human sciences, a descriptive analysis of the concepts of freedom, purpose, vision and normative value-commitments can be given, which is not inconsistent with factual-empirical inquiry into the cultural and historical conditions in which these realities emerge. To assume a complete dichotomy between the empirical-factual and the normative-valuational analysis is to perpetuate obscurantism. There is no inherent

logical incompatibility between the concept of 'empirical anthropology' and a reasonable descriptive 'philosophical anthropology.'
Any possibility of 'radical freedom' as the defining property of
human existence is ruled out as romantic moonshine.

The above account shows that Farber has successfully conceived
and suggested a fruitful alliance between phenomenology and naturalism through a critique of Husserl's philosophical writings in
the various stages of their development. His close acquaintance
with Husserl's works and a knowledge of the methodology of the
natural and social sciences have qualified him to develop, in the
course of his long philosophical career, the illuminating concept
and program of 'naturalistic phenomenology' on the principle of
the 'cooperation of methods.' To any dogmatic critics of such a
program he has to say that a:

"Truly descriptive view of attitudes and of interpretations of
existence is not opposed to causal analysis. It is misleading to have
what purports to be a descriptive view function as something supe-
rior to causal analysis. The methods for determining causes are
themselves descriptive. Hence, it is simply pretentious to speak of
rising above or digging beneath the methods of causal analysis and
of scientific description."[23] Such a naturalistic philosophy of robust
and well-informed common sense is bound to have a 'freeing' influence on the rigidity of many competing varieties of philosophical
postures reared on exclusive methods. Farber's naturalistic phenomenology is not committed to put an exclusive reliance on the
descriptive-phenomenological method and thus make the well nigh
impossible yet unnecessary effort to penetrate the depths of nature
through the narrow and thin aperture of the 'experience' of an
individual knower. No loss of prestige is involved for even the
most original and outstanding philosopher to make use of the
descriptive method in cooperation with the well-tested methods of
scientific inquiry with their standards of evidence, and supplemented by a judicious and reasonable use of the 'dialectic' method
according to which experience and inquiry are to be understood as
complex natural events occurring within and interacting with
specifiable social, cultural and organic conditions. The 'dialectic'
method, too, is not to be narrowly conceived as implying a one-

sided dependence of the 'superstructure' of our social, cultural, moral systems on the 'substructure' of our economic systems. Farber has made a lasting contribution to sound and healthy-minded philosophy based on the explicit recognition and judicious use of the principle of the 'cooperation and interaction of methods' functioning within a broad and pervasive naturalism.

Chapter X

EPILOGUE

OUR study in the philosophies of James, Dewey and Farber against the background of Husserl's 'pure phenomenology' has shown at one stroke the limitations of the ultra-rationalistic brand of transcendental phenomenology with its ambitious 'constitutive' program, and at the same time opened a new direction toward a naturalistic phenomenology. In the writings of James and Dewey, we have discovered strong tendencies and vague gropings toward such a consummation but not without inherent tensions. It is only in the writings of Farber who was nurtured both in the traditions of Husserlian phenomenology and American Naturalism and realism that we find a fully conscious and articulate development of Naturalistic phenomenology based on a competent critique of the subjectivistic and idealistic implications of Husserl's later writings. Husserl, James and Dewey, with all their varied background and training, share a common concern, namely the search for an *absolute beginning* in philosophy. [a] It is well known to critical students of the history of philosophy that whenever philosophers have been confronted with 'insoluble' conceptual problems they have invariably appealed to immediate experience. It was no different in the case of the 'unusual' trio Husserl, James and Dewey. It is another matter that they had their own concept of 'immediate experience.' We have attempted in the preceding chapters to delineate their philosophies of experience. Of the three, Husserl's genius represents the quintessence of the utopian quest for a radically 'presuppositionless' beginning in philosophy. A study in Husserl's phenomenology is a rewarding exercise in the utopian quest for an Ideal. Like all other Ideals, it brings out at once the value and the limitation of all utopian quests. Husserl's unflagging devotion to the rationalistic ideal shows at one stroke the *possibilities* and *limitations* of all human achievements. As is well-known,

130

Plato's *Republic* exercised such a double function in ancient Greece by showing the value as well as the limitation of the Spartan Ideal. Husserl with his *epoché* and the various 'reductions' remains a rigorous and 'pure' phenomenologist *par excellence*. Starting with pure experienced phenomena after having placed the whole world of nature and scientific findings within 'brackets,' he gained an awesome rigor with its alluring and yet impossible program of developing a 'pure' phenomenology and 'clarifying' all concepts in terms of the 'purified' experiences of an individual knower. This exclusive reliance on a monolithic method of phenomenological description and analysis gave him great 'freedom' to describe, clarify and reflectively analyze the essential structures of all kinds of experiences. And in this venture he attained significant successes—especially in the field of logic and mathematics. But the tragic flaw in this austere virtue of adhering to a single method of descriptive analysis of experience was that it enticed him slowly but surely into the most difficult, intricate and well-nigh impossible task of 'constituting' not only the *meaning* but also the actual world of natural and historical existence. Despite some of his outstanding achievements he always remained 'programmatic' and his promise outran his performance. The greater the distance between the two, the greater was his endeavor pursued with renewed vigor to arrive at the 'promised land.' The Ideal of a fully developed and completely 'clarified' 'Constitutive Phenomenology' in *all* the fields of experience beckoned him forward. But he realized the 'asymptotic' nature of the task and found himself almost alone in its pursuit. He became oblivious of the concrete world of natural and social existence and impervious to outside influences. The real, objective and factual problems ceased to interest him. He had to pay the price for the rigorous self-imposed discipline. The goal of deriving a reliable ontology through 'constitutive phenomenology' eluded him and seemed distant, and Husserl withdrew into the caverns of Transcendental Subjectivity with no return route in sight. Speaking of Husserl's awareness of the 'tedious' road and the 'infinite' work ahead during his last years, Farber says:

"As a powerful and virtually autonomous professor of philosophy (a *Geheimrat,* a title conferred by the first *Reich,* which he prized) and department head, Husserl was able to confine himself largely to intellectual relations with his subordinates and students, with most of his time available for his own meditations and productive work. It is small wonder, then, that a highly specialized vocabulary and an ingrown development should result, leaving for posterity a perpetual problem of interpretation."[1]

James came to philosophy *via* studies in physiology, psychology and medicine. His masterpiece, *The Principles of Psychology* deeply influenced Husserl and there are many common themes in the works of these two seminal thinkers. *The Principles of Psychology* shows a continuing tension between the causal-explanatory analysis of consciousness and the incipient phenomenological meaning-analysis of it. The *intentional* characteristic of consciousness mentioned by James referred to its directedness to a real historical object and *not* to a *meant* object as in the case of Husserl. There is no fully articulate 'phenomenological reduction' of the Husserlian type in James but there is a strong undercurrent of the *Lebenswelt* type of reduction to 'immediate experience.' The credit for hitting upon the concept of 'pure intentionality' as the essential and defining property of consciousness in the sense of its directedness to *meant* objectivities, belongs to Husserl. Consequently, whereas we have a *transcendental analysis* of the cognitive relation in Husserl implying the *necessary truth* that the very concept of a conscious act involves the concept of its object (intentional or meant object), in James' psychology and philosophy we have illuminating descriptive analyses of consciousness and various concepts in terms of 'lived' immediate experience. If therefore, there was a lack of Husserlian rigor in James' writings there was a corresponding gain which kept him relatively free from the subjectivistic and idealistic entanglement of the later Husserl. James had neither the temperament nor the willingness to conjure up the ultra-rationalistic vision of a completely systematized and unified philosophy based on apodictic certainty—which had inspired Husserl.[2] James' practical experience in physiology and psychology made him adopt the healthy 'principle of complementarity' in the explanation of consciousness. He almost gave the impression of wavering between the causal-explanatory and the descriptive-phenomenological methods. When James turned to philosophy from his psychological studies he found the philosophical world riddled with all kinds of conceptual confusions. As we have shown above, James hit upon the now famous 'pragmatic method' together with the method of 'radical empiricism,' and appealed to what he termed 'pure experience' for a clarification of important philosophical concepts. His concepts of 'pure experience' and 'clarification' were, however, different from those of Husserl. James, as we have indicated in the course of our studies, gave illuminating analyses of the concepts of, 'self,' 'knowledge,' 'meaning,' 'truth,' and 'reality' in terms of their *evidences* in 'pure' pre-reflective immediate experience. This phenomenological procedure of validating *all* concepts in terms of immediate experience was the binding link between his pragmatism and his radical empiricism—though James failed to see it. When accused of subjectivism and idealism, James reacted sharply, not without exasperation. His studies in anatomy, physiology, medicine, and evolutionary biology qualified him to take the natural 'body' seriously and give it a central place both in psychology and philosophy. He constantly endeavored to establish *real* connections between man and the natural world through the adoption of both the causal-genetic and descriptive methods.[3] His first-hand acquaintance with experimental science left a lasting impression on his philosophical thinking and consequently he rejected the charge of subjectivism against him. He wrote:

"A real science of man is now being built up out of the theory of evolution and the facts of archeology, the nervous system and the senses."[4]

Again emphasized James:

"I conceive realities as existent, as having existed, or about to exist, in absolute independence of my thought of them."[5]

And yet when all this is said and done his concept of 'pure experience' remained ambiguous. His attempt to penetrate the structure of reality through the phenomenologically described traits of human experience with the aid of a watered down criterion of 'rationality,' and his philosophical *practice* of relying exclusively on descriptive analysis of experience landed him in insuperable difficulties and made him vulnerable to the charges of subjectivism. Consequently we see James branching out into the border-line areas of psychical research, mysticism and other varieties of religious experience. No wonder James wavered, and failed to make full use of 'methodological pluralism' in his philosophy as he had attempted to do in his psychology. Once again an *absolute* beginning with 'pure experience' had proved abortive for the purposes of a reliable ontology. However, James remains a precursor of an American brand of naturalistic phenomenology.

Dewey marks an advance over James in the direction toward a naturalistic phenomenology. He, like Husserl, was immensely influenced by James' *Principles of Psychology* but, unlike Husserl, he endeavored to assimilate James' insights within the framework of naturalism. Dewey, though he was not a practicing scientist like James, took the lessons of evolutionary biology and the import of the experimental method of inquiry more seriously, and worked out the implications of both for philosophy in a more conscious and deliberate manner. And yet, he, like Husserl and James, turned to 'immediate experience' for solving the tangled conceptual problems of philosophy. No doubt this concept of 'immediate experience' as *transactional* (a product of dynamic interaction between a live organism and a changing natural and social environment) with its unifying *pervasive quality* proved more fruitful. Experience was constituted by 'doing-and-undergoing' and was not a 'thin' affair occurring somewhere 'in' the mind of the knower, but had a 'depth' reaching into the background of nature. Dewey gave interesting analyses of esthetic experience, moral experience and the cognitive experience of knowledge, truth and inquiry—all within the naturalistic framework. The key concept of his philosophy of experience—in all its varieties—was found by us to be that of the *pervasive* integrating quality of the experienced situation. Dewey endeavored to 'penetrate' nature through a descriptive analysis of this pervasive quality. We have seen how this approach had serious limitations and Dewey was aware of the circularity involved in constructing a realistic ontology of Nature through this 'window' of the experienced quality of a situation. This pervasive quality of the experienced situation was the *absolute beginning* for Dewey—the 'given' for his philosophical reflection. And once again an exclusive dependence on a single descriptive method of phenomenological analysis of experience in Dewey's *actual* philosophical procedure led to an impasse.

Drawing upon the insights of Husserl, James, Dewey and Whitehead, Farber has made a conscious and deliberate use of the principle of 'ontological monism' coupled with 'methodological pluralism' in order to arrive at a satisfactory ontology of nature. His pervasive naturalism makes no pretense of an *absolute* beginning. The very concepts of an absolute presuppositionless beginning and of the 'given' are critically examined. For a reflective thinker his immediate experience may mark a beginning. It is the 'given' for him. But we should ask: Who is this individual thinker? Is he absolute? Is he not a concrete person born of his parents, occupying a finite span of time and space, and conditioned by natural, organic and social-historical factors? Once it is recognized that the concept of 'beginning' or the 'given' is relative to the *problem* at hand, and that specific problems require specific methods to solve them, the strange fascination for and the uncanny spell of 'absolute beginning' in philosophizing wears thin. Neither Husserl, nor James, nor Dewey was able to cast off the mystic charm of making such an absolute beginning. It is to the lasting credit of Farber to ease such a *tense* search for a presuppositionless beginning. We have tried to show in the previous chapter that Farber escapes the subjectivistic consequences of beginning with the *experience* of an individual knower, and places the phenomenological description of experience in the proper context of general methodology in which other methods such as experimental inquiry, dialectical method of social-historical analysis, language analysis, and formal-conceptual analysis all play their legitimate role for a total understanding of man and his place in nature. His naturalism takes care of the ontological monism of natural-physical events together with the descriptively determined and discovered traits which emerge at various levels of organization–physical, organic, social and cultural. All events are located within nature, and no conflict is seen between a phenomenological analysis of our value-experiences and their causal-empirical analysis in terms of social-historical conditions. Both are required for adequate understanding. Farber has therefore performed the historical function of 'containing' the 'irrational' off-shoots of phenomenology in the various forms of 'existentialism,' retained a cherished place for phenomenological-analysis within general methodology, and worked out the program of an adequately supported American brand of Naturalistic phenomenology by drawing out the implications of a trend already discernible in the writings of James and Dewey. Nothing less was demanded by a sane and healthy-minded philosophy reared on the well-grounded findings of the sciences, and the human and humane interests of mankind.

BIBLIOGRAPHY

A. MAJOR WORKS OF WILLIAM JAMES

The Principles of Psychology, Henry Holt and Co., 1927, 2 vols. 1890.
The Will to Believe and Other Essays in Popular Philosophy, Longmans, Green and Co., New York, 1897.
The Varieties of Religious Experience, The New American Library, New York, 1958 (1902).
Pragmatism, The World Publishing Company, Cleveland, Ohio, 1955 (1907).
The Meaning of Truth, Longmans, Green and Co., New York, 1909.
A Pluralistic Universe, Longmans, Green and Co., New York, 1943 (1909).
Some Problems of Philosophy, Longmans, Green and Co., New York, 1948 (1911). Posthumous, ed., by Henry James, Jr.
Essays in Radical Empiricism, Longmans, Green and Co., New York, 1938, 1943, 1947 (1912). Posthumous, ed. by R. B. Perry.
Collected Essays and Reviews, Longmans, Green and Co., New York, 1920. Posthumous, ed., by R. B. Perry.
William James on Psychical Research, The Viking Press, New York, 1960. Posthumous, ed. by Gardner Murphy and Robert O. Ballou.

B. MAJOR WORKS OF JOHN DEWEY

Studies in Logical Theory, The University of Chicago Press, Chicago, 1903.
The Influence of Darwin on Philosophy and Other Essays in Contemporary Thought, Henry Holt and Co., New York, 1910.
How We Think, D. C. Heath and Co., Boston, 1910.
Essays in Experimental Logic, The University of Chicago Press, Chicago, 1916.
Reconstruction in Philosophy, Henry Holt and Co., New York, 1920. (Enlarged edition with a new introduction, The New American Library, New York, 1951.)
Experience and Nature, W. W. Norton and Co., New York, 1929. (Dover Publications, Inc., New York, 1958.)
The Quest for Certainty, Minton, Balch and Co., New York, 1929. (Capricorn Books, New York, 1960.)
Philosophy and Civilization, Minton, Balch and Co., New York, 1931. (Capricorn Books, New York, 1963.)
Art as Experience, Minton, Balch and Co., New York, 1934.
Experience and Education, Macmillan Co., New York, 1938.
Logic: The Theory of Inquiry, Henry Holt and Co., New York, 1939.

"Theory of Valuation" (monograph), *International Encyclopedia of Unified Science*, vol. II, no. 4, The University of Chicago Press, Chicago, 1939.
Problems of Men, Philosophical Library, New York, 1946.
"Some Implications of Anti-Intellectualisms," *Journal of Philosophy*, vii, Sept. 1, 1910.
"Classicism as an Evangel," *Journal of Philosophy*, XVIII, Nov. 24, 1921.
"Realism Without Monism or Dualism," *Journal of Philosophy*, XIX, June 22, 1922.
"Some Comments of Philosophical Discussion," *Journal of Philosophy*, XXI, April 10, 1924.
"In Reply to Some Criticisms," *Journal of Philosophy*, XXVI, May 8, 1930.
"An Empirical Account of Appearance," *Journal of Philosophy*, XXIV, August 18, 1927.
"Unity of Science as a Social Problem," *Encyclopaedia of Unified Science*, I, no. 1, The University of Chicago Press, Chicago, 1938.
"The Field of Value," *Value: A Cooperative Inquiry* (ed. Lepley, Ray), Columbia University Press, 1949.
"The Need for a Recovery of Philosophy," *Creative Intelligence: Essays in the Pragmatic Attitude*, John Dewey and Others, Henry Holt and Co., 1917.
"Aesthetic Experience as a Primary Phase and as an Artistic Development," *The Journal of Aesthetics and Art-Criticism*, IX, Sept. 1950, 56-58.

C. MAJOR WORKS OF MARVIN FARBER

Phenomenology as a Method and as a Philosophical Discipline, University of Buffalo Publications in Philosophy, 1928.
Philosophical Essays in Memory of Edmund Husserl, Harvard University Press, Cambridge, 1940. (Editor and Co-author.)
The Foundation of Phenomenology, third edition, State University of New York Press, Albany, 1967.
Editor and Co-author, *Philosophic Thought in France and the United States*, second edition, State University of New York Press, Albany, 1968.
Naturalism and Subjectivism, State University of New York Press, Albany, 1968.
The Aims of Phenomenology, Harper and Row Torchbooks, New York, 1966.
Phenomenology and Existence, Harper and Row Torchbooks, New York, 1967.
Basic Issues of Philosophy, Harper and Row Torchbooks, New York, 1968.
"Toward a Naturalistic Philosophy of Experience," *Diogenes*, no. 60, Paris, 1967, pp. 103-129.

D. MAJOR WORKS OF EDMUND HUSSERL

Logische Untersuchungen, Max Niemeyer, Halle, 1900-1901.
The Idea of Phenomenology, translated by William P. Alston and George Nakhnikian, Martinus Nijhoff, The Hague, 1964.
"Philosophy as Rigorous Science" in Quentin Lauer, *Edmund Husserl: Phenomenology and the Crisis of Philosophy*, Harper and Row, New York, 1965, pp. 69-147.
Ideas: General Introduction to Pure Phenomenology, translated by W. R. Boyce Gibson, Collier Books, New York, 1962.
"Phenomenology," *Encyclopaedia Brittanica*, 14th ed., London, 1927, vol. 17, col. 699-702.

Cartesian Meditations: An Introduction to Phenomenology, translated by Dorion Cairns, Martinus Nijhoff, The Hague, 1960.
Formale und transzendentale Logik, Max Niemeyer, Halle, 1929.
Erfahrung und Urteil, edited by L. Landgrebe, Academia Verlag, Prague, 1939.

E. OTHER RELEVANT WORKS

Ames, V. M., "John Dewey as Aesthetician," *The Journal of Aesthetics and Art-Criticism,* XII, no. 2, Dec. 1953, 145-168.
————, "Expression and Aesthetic Experience," *Ibid.,* vol. VI, no. 2, Dec. 1947, 172-179.
Ayer, A. J., *Language, Truth and Logic,* 2nd ed., Victor Gollancz, Ltd., London, 1948.
Black, Max, ed., *Philosophy in America,* Cornell University, Ithaca, N. Y. 1965.
Boas, George, "Communication in Dewey's Aesthetics," *The Journal of Aesthetics and Art-Criticism,* XII, no. 12, Dec. 1953, 177-183.
Capek, Millic, "The Reappearance of the Self in the Last Philosophy of William James," *Philosophical Review,* Oct. 1953.
Chapman, Harmon, "Realism and Phenomenology," in *The Return to Reason,* ed., by John Wild, Henry Regnery Co., Chicago, 1953.
Collingwood, R. G., *The Principles of Art,* The Clarendon Press, Oxford, 1938.
Croce, Benedetto, *Aesthetic,* 2nd ed., Macmillan Co., London, 1922.
Croce, Benedetto, "Dewey's Aesthetics and the Theory of Knowledge," *The Journal of Aesthetics and Art-Criticism,* XI, no. 1, Sept. 1952.
————, "On the Aesthetics of Dewey," *Ibid.,* VI, 1948, 203-207.
Ducasse, C. J., *Art, The Critics, and You,* Oskar Piest, New York, 1944.
Edie, James M., ed., *An Invitation to Phenomenology,* Chicago, 1965.
————, ed., *Phenomenology in America,* Quadrangle Books, Chicago, 1967.
Ghiselin, Brewster, ed., *The Creative Process,* The New American Library, New York, 1955.
Gilbert, Katherine, and Kuhn, Helmut, *A History of Aesthetics,* 2nd ed., Indiana University Press, Bloomington, 1953.
Gurwitsch, Aron, *Studies in Phenomenological Psychology,* Northwestern University Press, Evanston, 1966.
James, Henry, Jr., ed., *The Letters of William James,* 2 vols., Atlantic Monthly Press, Boston, 1920.
Kockelmans, Joseph J., ed., *Phenomenology: The Philosophy of Edmund Husserl and Its Interpretation,* Doubleday and Company, Inc., Garden City, New York, 1967.
Lamont, Corliss, ed., *Dialogue on John Dewey,* Horizon Press, New York, 1959.
Linschoten, Hans, *On the Way Toward a Phenomenological Psychology,* edited by Amedeo Giorgi, Duquesne University Press, Pittsburgh, Pa., 1968.
McDermott, John J., ed., *The Writings of William James,* The Modern Library, New York, 1968.
Mathur, D. C., "A Note on the Concept of 'Consummatory Experience' in Dewey's Aesthetics," *The Journal of Philosophy,* vol. LXIII, no. 9, April 28, 1966, pp. 225-231.
Ogden, C. K., and Richards, I. A., *The Meaning of Meaning,* Harcourt, Brace and Co., Inc., New York, 1923.

Pepper, S. C., "The Concept of Fusion in Dewey's Aesthetic Theory," *The Journal of Aesthetics and Art-Criticism*, XIII, no. 2, Dec. 1953, 169-176.

Perry, R. B., *The Thought and Character of William James*, 2 vols. Little, Brown and Co., Boston, 1935.

————, *In the Spirit of William James*, Yale University Press, New Haven, 1938.

————, *General Theory of Value*, Longmans, Green, and Co., New York, 1926.

————, *Realms of Value*, Harvard University Press, Cambridge, 1954.

Ryle, Gilbert, *The Concept of Mind*, Barnes and Noble, Inc., New York, 1949.

Santayana, George, "Dewey's Naturalistic Metaphysics," *Obiter Scripta*, Charles Scribner's Sons, New York, 1936.

Schilpp, Paul Arthur, ed., *The Philosophy of John Dewey*, The Library of Living Philosophers, vol. 1, Chicago, 1939.

Schutz, Alfred, "William James' Concept of the Stream of Consciousness Phenomenologically Interpreted," *Philosophy and Phenomenological Research*, vol. I, no. 4, 1941.

Spiegelberg, H., *The Phenomenological Movement: An Historical Introduction*, vols. I and II, M. Nijhoff, The Hague, 1960.

Stevenson, C. L., *Ethics and Language*, Yale University Press, New Haven, 1944.

————, *Facts and Values*, Yale University Press, New Haven, 1963.

Stevenson, C. L., "The Emotive Meaning of Ethical Terms," *Mind*, 1937.

Thévenaz, Pierre, *What Is Phenomenology?*, Quadrangle Books, Inc., Chicago, 1962.

Vivas, Eliseo, and Krieger, Murray, eds., *The Problems of Aesthetics*, Rinehart, New York, 1953.

Whitehead, A. N., *Science and the Modern World*, The New American Library, New York, 1948.

Wild, John, *Existence and the World of Freedom*, Englewood Cliffs, 1963.

————, *The Radical Empiricism of William James*, Doubleday and Company, Inc., Garden City, New York, 1969.

Wilson, Gay, *William James*, The Viking Press, New York, 1967.

Wilshire, Bruce, *William James and Phenomenology*, Indiana University Press, Bloomington, 1968.

Wittgenstein, Ludwig, *Tractatus Logico-Philosophicus*, translated by O. F. Pears and B. F. McGuinness, Routledge and Kegan Paul, London, 1961.

————, *Philosophical Investigations*, German text and English translation by G. E. M. Anscombe, Basil Blackwell, Oxford, 1953.

NOTES

CHAPTER I

1. Cf. (a) Aron Gurwitsch, "William James' Theory of the 'Transitive Parts' of the Stream of Consciousness" in *Studies in Phenomenological Psychology*, Evanston, 1966.
   (b) Alfred Schutz, "William James' Concept of the Stream of Consciousness, Phenomenologically Interpreted," *Philosophy and Phenomenological Research*, No. 4, vol. I, 1941.
   (c) James M. Edie, "Notes on the Philosophical Anthropology of William James" in *An Invitation to Phenomenology*, edited by James M. Edie, Chicago, 1965.
   (d) John Wild, *Existence and the World of Freedom*, Englewood Cliffs, 1963, *passim*.
   (e) John Wild, *The Radical Empiricism of William James*, Doubleday and Company, Inc., New York, 1969, *passim*.
   (f) Hans Linschoten, *On the Way Toward a Phenomenological Psychology*, edited by Amedeo Giorgi, Duquesne University Press, Pittsburgh, Pa., 1968.
   (g) Bruce Wilshire, *William James and Phenomenology*, Indiana University Press, Bloomington, 1968.
2. William James, *Pragmatism*, The World Publishing Company, Cleveland, Ohio, 1955, p. 14.
3. In the Logos essay Husserl, bemoaning the fact that the goals and methods of philosophy have not been clarified and distinguished from those of the empirical sciences of nature, says,
   "Thus philosophy, according to its historical purpose the loftiest and most rigorous of all sciences, representing as it does humanity's imperishable demand for *pure* and *absolute knowledge* . . . , is incapable of assuming the form of rigorous science" (emphasis mine). (*Phenomenology and the Crisis of Philosophy*, tr. Quentin Lauer, Harper and Row, New York, 1965, p. 72).
   Further, Husserl anticipates his later doctrines of *epoché*, 'intentionality,' and the scientific 'absolute' and 'objective' nature of essential knowledge, as well as his thesis of regarding being as a correlate of consciousness, in the same essay. The following passages show that the germs of 'transcendental' idealism were present in the Logos essay which truly was a turning point in the philosophical career of Husserl:
   "It also becomes clear that just as every scientific, so every prescientific application of nature *must in principle remain excluded in a theory of knowledge that is to retain its univocal sense. So, too, must all expressions that*

141

imply thetic existential positings of things in the framework of space, time, causality, etc. This obviously applies also to all existential positings with regard to the empirical being of the investigator, of his psychical faculties, and the like" (emphasis mine) (*op. cit.*, p. 89). Again,

"Further: if knowledge theory will nevertheless investigate the problems of the relationship between consciousness and being, *it can have before its eyes only being as the correlate of consciousness,* as something 'intended' after the manner of consciousness: as perceived, remembered, expected, represented, pictorially imagined, identified, distinguished, believed, opined, evaluated, etc. It is clear, then that the investigation must be directed toward a scientific essential knowledge of consciousness, toward that which consciousness itself 'is' according to its essence in all its distinguishable forms." (*op. cit.*, p. 89) (emphasis mine).

4. Marvin Farber, *The Foundation of Phenomenology*, State University of New York Press, Albany, 1967, p. 17.

5. *Ideas*, Tr. W. R. Boyce Gibson, Collier Macmillan Ltd., London, 1967, pp. 99-100.

6. *Op. cit.*, p. 153.

7. *Op. cit.*, p. 139.

8. *Cartesian Meditations*, Tr. Dorion Cairns, Martinus Nijhoff, The Hague, 1960, p. 84.

9. M. Farber, *Phenomenology and Existence*, Harper Torchbooks, Harper and Row, New York, 1967, p. 101.

10. *The Foundation of Phenomenology*, State University of New York Press, Albany, 1967, p. 535.

11. Cf. R. B. Perry, *In the Spirit of William James* (Yale University Press, New Haven, 1938), pp. 75-123. Perry brings out the various stages of progress in James' conception of experience—the psychological, the phenomenological (the stage of "pure experience") and the metaphysical. The last stage, Perry points out, was advanced in later years by James under the influence of Bergson. However, whether James elevated "experience" to the status of a metaphysical reality, and if so in what sense, is a controversial point. It is possible to interpret James' 'pure experience' in two senses: (i) the flow of human experience and (ii) the whole of natural reality.

12. In his *Pragmatism* (1907) W. James wrote, "But one thing that has *counted* so far in philosophy is that a man should *see* things, see them straight in his own peculiar way, and be dissatisfied with any opposite way of seeing them" (emphasis is original) (p. 20). The page reference is to the Meridian Books edition of *Pragmatism* (The World Publishing Company, Cleveland, 1963).

13. Marvin Farber, *Basic Issues of Philosophy* (New York: Harper and Row, 1968), p. 121.

This book (his latest in Harper and Row publications—his earlier books in the series being *The Aims of Phenomenology*, 1966 and *Phenomenology and Existence*, 1967) is the result of the author's long and mature experience in philosophizing. Its dominant note of "pervasive naturalism" is meant to counteract the "pervasive subjectivism" of Husserl's transcendental idealism. His personal relation to E. Husserl and his first hand acquaintance with his thought have qualified him immensely to see both the merits of Husserl's descriptive phenomenology and the limitations and weaknesses of his transcendental idealism. With characteristic boldness he has rescued the essential insights of Husserl from the "romantic" and "non-rational" turn given to phenomenology by some of the "so-called" followers of Husserl both in Europe and America. The main tenor of M. Farber's assessment of Phenomenology in its long and chequered career will be evident from the following: "Freed from its idealistic encumbrances, it may assist the examination of theories of existence, and promote a thoroughgoing critical attitude. In this respect it is a helpful auxiliary method, serving scientific method in the broadest sense" (*Basic Issues of Philosophy*, p. 104).

14. John Dewey, *Experience and Nature* (New York: W. W. Norton and Co., 1929), p. 4a.
15. *The Principles of Psychology*, vol. I, p. 271.
16. *Op. cit.*, p. 272.
17. *The Principles of Psychology*, vol. I, p. 245.
18. Cf. J. Dewey's essay on "Qualitative Thought" in *Philosophy and Civilization* (New York: Minton Balch and Co., 1931).
18a. This may be interpreted to mean that James had abandoned naturalistic realism. However, his language is ambiguous on this point. In one mode of expression the object is what it reveals itself to be in experience, in another mode it is the real, historical object which is given in experience. James failed to see the tension between these two positions.
19. R. B. Perry, *In the Spirit of William James*, New Haven: Yale University Press, 1938), p. 78.
20. W. James, *Essays in Radical Empiricism* (New York: Longmans, Green and Co., 1943), p. 42.
21. "Does 'Consciousness' Exist?," *Essays in Radical Empiricism*, p. 2.
22. *Op. cit.*, pp. 3-4.
23. *Op. cit.*, p. 4.
24. *Op. cit.*, p. 25.
25. *Op. cit.*, pp. 23-24.
26. *Op. cit.*, pp. 26-27.
27. *Op. cit.*, p. 27.
28. *Op. cit.*, p. 34.
29. *Op. cit.*, p. 36.
30. "The Place of Affectional Facts in a World of Pure Experience," *Essays in Radical Empiricism*, p. 139.
31. *Op. cit.*, p. 144.
32. *Op. cit.*, p. 150.
33. "The Experience of Activity," *Essays in Radical Empiricism*, pp. 159-60.

CHAPTER II

1. *The Foundation of Phenomenology*, State University of New York Press, Albany, N. Y., 1967, p. 554.
2. Marvin Farber in his *Phenomenology and Existence*, Harper Torchbooks, Harper and Row, New York, 1967, pp. 104-112 shows how Husserl slips

from phenomenology to ontology through an artificial *epoché* and posits the transcendental knower in contradistinction from the mundane experient. He writes, "As a matter of fact, it is not *possible* to remove the mundane psyche, the knower from the world; just as it is not possible to have a solitary ego who can exist apart from other egos, or the world of culture" (p. 105).

Further, "The absolute justification which Husserl seeks by way of his apodictic critique could only yield ideal abstractions, not even pinpoints in the real, natural world in which we actually live. The ontology reared upon the *epoché*, with all the 'purification' introduced, is something *Sui generis;* it cannot be the real ontology which alone can satisfy the demands of experience by conforming to its accumulated and warranted knowledge" (p. 111-112).

3. *The Principles of Psychology*, vol. I, p. 291.
4. *Op. cit.*, p. 350.
5. *Op. cit.*, p. 364-5.
6. *Op. cit.*, p. 369-70.
7. *Op. cit.*, p. 296.
8. *Op. cit.*, p. 296.
9. *Op. cit.*, p. 297.
10. *Op. cit.*, p. 297-8.
11. *Op. cit.*, p. 298.
12. *Op. cit.*, p. 299.
13. *Op. cit.*, p. 300.
14. *Op. cit.*, p. 305.
15. *Op. cit.*, p. 331-2.
16. *Op. cit.*, p. 332.
17. *Op. cit.*, p. 333.
18. *Op. cit.*, p. 334.
19. *Op. cit.*, p. 335.
20. *Op. cit.*, p. 336.
21. *Op. cit.*, p. 338.
22. *Op. cit.*, p. 339.
23. *Op. cit.*, footnote, p. 341.
24. *Op. cit.*, p. 341.
25. *Op. cit.*, p. 371.
26. *Op. cit.*, p. 372-3.
27. *Essays in Radical Empiricism and a Pluralistic Universe*, Longmans, Green and Co., New York, 1943, p. 2.
28. *Op. cit.*, p. 3-4.
29. *Op. cit.*, p. 4.
30. *Op. cit.*, p. 23.
31. *Op. cit.*, p. 23-4.
32. *Op. cit.*, p. 37.
33. *Essays in Radical Empiricism*, p. 43.
34. *Op. cit.*, p. 48.
35. "Is Life Worth Living?," *The Will to Believe, and Other Essays in Popular Philosophy*, Longmans, Green and Co., New York, 1897, p. 51.
36. "What Psychical Research Has Accomplished?," *Op. cit.*, p. 321.

CHAPTER III

1. On this, see the interesting thesis of J. Dewey in his essay "The Significance of the Problem of Knowledge," in *The Influence of Darwin on Philosophy and Other Essays in Contemporary Thought* (New York: Henry Holt and Co., 1910), pp. 271-304.

2. Cf. M. Farber's suggestive and illuminating chapter on "Experience and the Problems of Philosophy" in his *Basic Issues of Philosophy* (New York: Harper and Row, 1968), pp. 66-97. He has discussed at length the various ways in which philosophical problems may arise and put forward criteria for distinguishing between the genuine and the spurious.

3. Reprinted in *The Meaning of Truth* (New York: Longmans, Green, and Co., 1909), p. 1.

4. *Op. cit.,* p. 3.

5. *The Principles of Psychology,* vol. I, p. 288.

6. *Essays in Radical Empiricism,* chapter VI.

7. "The Experience of Activity" in *Essays in Radical Empiricism,* pp. 159-60.

8. *Op. cit.,* p. 163.

9. *Op. cit.,* p. 166.

10. *Op. cit.,* p. 168.

11. *Op. cit.,* pp. 170-171, footnote.

12. From an unpublished letter in the James Collection in the Widener Library, Harvard University, quoted by R. B. Perry in *In the Spirit of William James* (New Haven: Yale University Press, 1938), p. 58.

13. "A World of Pure Experience" in *Essays in Radical Empiricism,* p. 53.

14. James had discussed this problem of "knowledge—about" also in his earlier articles on "The Function of Cognition," *Mind,* vol. X, 1885, and "The Tigers in India," *Psychological Review,* vol. II, p. 105 (1895) and reprinted in *The Meaning of Truth,* pp. 1-50.

15. "Essence of Humanism," in *The Meaning of Truth,* p. 127.

16. "Does Consciousness Exist?" in *Essays in Radical Empiricism,* p. 9.

17. *Op. cit.,* p. 9-10.

18. *Op. cit.,* p. 12-13.

19. It may be historically more exact to say with R. B. Perry that James never wholly forgot his early naturalistic position despite some of the doubts that we have raised about his later writings involving an interpretation of his conception of "pure experience" and his interests in "mystical" and "psychical" experiences.

20. *Op. cit.,* p. 15.

21. *Op. cit.,* p. 16. James affirmed the same position in his *The Meaning of Truth,* pp. 42, 195, note; *A Pluralistic Universe,* p. 339-340; *Some Problems of Philosophy,* pp. 50-57, 67-70.

22. *Some Problems of Philosophy* (New York: Longmans, Green and Co., 1928), p. 106.

23. "Humanism and Truth," in *The Meaning of Truth,* p. 58-9.

24. *The Meaning of Truth,* pp. 1-42.

25. *Op. cit.,* pp. 43-50.

26. *Essays in Radical Empiricism.*

27. "The Tigers in India," in *The Meaning of Truth,* pp. 44-5.
28. "The Function of Cognition," in *The Meaning of Truth,* pp. 1-42, passim.
29. "A World of Pure Experience," in *Essays in Radical Empiricism,* p. 56.
30. *Op. cit.,* p. 57.
31. *Op. cit.,* p. 61.
32. *Op. cit.,* p. 59.
33. *Op. cit.,* p. 74-5.
34. *Op. cit.,* p. 78.
35. *Op. cit.,* p. 79-80.
36. *Op. cit.,* p. 80. Cf. also "The Tigers in India," in *The Meaning of Truth,* pp. 49-50.
37. *The Meaning of Truth,* p. 185.
38. *Pragmatism* (New York: The World Publishing Company, 1963), p. 45.
39. *Op. cit.,* p. 46.
40. *The Meaning of Truth,* p. 221.
41. *Op. cit.,* p. 234.
42. *Op. cit.,* p. 235.
43. Preface to *The Meaning of Truth,* p. vi.
44. *Op. cit.,* p. vi, vii.
45. "Humanism and Truth," in *The Meaning of Truth,* p. 82.
46. *Op. cit.,* p. 84-5.
47. *Op. cit.,* p. 86.

CHAPTER IV

1. "The Experience of Activity," *Essays in Radical Empiricism,* p. 160.
2. *The Will to Believe and Other Essays,* Longmans, Green and Co., New York, 1897, pp. 63-110.
3. *Collected Essays and Reviews,* Longmans, Green and Co., New York, 1920, pp. 43-68.
4. *Op. cit.,* Preface, p. ix.
4. (a) *Op. cit.*
5. *Collected Essays and Reviews,* pp. 67-8.
6. "The Sentiment of Rationality," *The Will to Believe and Other Essays,* p. 63.
7. *Op. cit.,* p. 64.
8. *Op. cit.,* p. 66.
9. *Op. cit.,* p. 73.
10. *Op. cit.,* p. 75.
11. *Op. cit.,* p. 82.
12. Cf. "Reflex Action and Theism," *The Will to Believe and Other Essays,* p. 125
13. "Hegel and His Method," *A Pluralistic Universe,* Longmans, Green, and Co., New York, 1943, p. 113-4.
14. James admits the influence of Bergson on him in his repudiation of "Vicious Intellectualism." Cf. "Bergson and His Critics," *op. cit., passim.*
15. *Op. cit.,* p. 112.
16. *Op. cit.,* p. 113.
17. "The Perception of Reality," *The Principles of Psychology,* vol. II, 1890, p. 283.
18. *Op. cit.,* p. 288-9.

19. *Op. cit.*, p. 293.
20. *Op. cit.*, p. 294.
21. *Op. cit.*, p. 295.
22. *Op. cit.*, p. 297.
23. *Op. cit.*, p. 297.
24. *Op. cit.*, p. 301.
25. *Op. cit.*, p. 301.
26. Footnote, *Op. cit.*, p. 302.
27. *Op. cit.*, p. 312.
28. *Op. cit.*, p. 317.
29. *Op. cit.*, p. 317.
30. *Op. cit.*
31. *A Pluralistic Universe*, p. 305.
32. *Op. cit.*, p. 307.
33. *Op. cit.*, p. 311.
34. *Op. cit.*, p. 314-5.
35. *Op. cit.*, p. 321.
36. *Varieties of Religious Experience*, p. 393.
37. *Op. cit.*, p. 394.
38. *Op. cit.*, p. 394-5.
39. "On Some Hegeligism," *The Will to Believe*, pp. 294-298.
40. "A Suggestion About Mysticism," *Collected Essays and Reviews*, p. 500.
41. *Op. cit.*, p. 500.
42. *Op. cit.*, p. 503.

CHAPTER V

(a) James' theory of "pure experience" and of "truth" was not intended by him to be a subjective one. He recognized the independent structure of reality (named by him "pure experience") without surrendering the dynamic and interested character of mind. This is borne out amply in one of his most lucid letters where he likens the world metaphorically to a cast of beans on a table. He says,

"By themselves they (the beans) spell nothing. An onlooker may group them as he likes. He may simply count them all and map them. He may select groups and name them capriciously, or name them to suit certain extrinsic purposes of his. Whatever he does, so long as he *takes account of them,* his account is neither false nor irrelevant. If neither, why not call it true. It *fits* the beans—*minus*—him, and expresses the *total* fact or beans—*plus*—him. Truth in this total sense is partially ambiguous, then. If he simply counts or maps, he obeys a subjective interest as much as if he traces figures. Let that stand for pure "intellectual" treatment of the beans, while grouping them variously stands for non-intellectual interests. All that Schiller and I contend for is that there is *no* 'truth' without *some* interest, and that non-intellectual interests play a part as well as intellectual ones" (W. James, *The Letters of William James,* ed. Henry James, Boston: The Atlantic Monthly Press, 1920, II, 295).

1. "Does Consciousness Exist?," *Essays in Radical Empiricism and a Pluralistic Universe,* Longmans, Green and Co., New York, 1943, pp. 26-7.

148   NATURALISTIC PHILOSOPHIES OF EXPERIENCE

2. John Dewey, "The Development of American Pragmatism," *Philosophy and Civilization* (New York, Capricorn Books, 1963), p. 28.
3. John Dewey, "Experience, Knowledge and Value—A Rejoinder," *The Philosophy of John Dewey*, ed. Paul Arthur Schilpp (New York, Tudor Publishing Co., 1951), p. 533, n. 16.
4. John Dewey, *Experience and Nature* (New York, Dover Publications, Inc., 1958), p. 3-4.
5. *Experience and Nature*, p. 29.
6. *Ibid.*, p. 6.
7. *Ibid.*, p. 31.
8. *Ibid.*, p. 37.
9. *Ibid.*, p. 37.
10. *Ibid.*, p. 37-8.
10. (a) However, in Dewey's concept of the *pervasive quality* of an experienced situation, one can discern an incipient and implicit concern with such a beginning in philosophizing. This will be evident from what follows.
11. J. Dewey, *Reconstruction in Philosophy*, Beacon Press, Boston, 1967.
12. See George Santayana, "Dewey's Naturalistic Metaphysics," *Obiter Scripta*, Charles Scribner's Sons, New York, 1936, pp. 213-240.
13. *Experience and Nature*, p. 17-8.
14. *Experience and Nature*, p. 18.
15. On this see further his
    (a) *Studies in Logical Theory*, Chicago: The University of Chicago Press, 1903, p. 72.
    (b) The Quest for Certainty, John Dewey, Minton, Balch and Co., New York, 1929, p. 275.
    (c) John Dewey, "Some Implications of Anti-Intellectualisms," *Journal of Philosophy*, VII, Sept. 1, 1910, p. 479.
    (d) John Dewey, "Classicism as an Evangel," *Journal of Philosophy*, XVIII, Nov. 24, 1921, p. 666.
16. *Experience and Nature*, p. x.
17. *Ibid.*, p. 3a.
18. *Ibid.*, p. 3a.
19. *Art as Experience*, Minton, Balch and Co., New York, 1934, p. 194.
20. *Ibid.*, p. 195.
    On this point Dewey draws upon James' notion of the stream of consciousness with its "focus" and "fringe," and its "flights" and "perches." Cf. *Experience and Nature*, pp. 311-12.
21. *Experience and Nature*, pp. 4a-1.
22. *Ibid.*, pp. 3-4.
22. (a) Dewey says, ". . . things are objects to be treated, used, acted upon and with, enjoyed and endured, even more than things to be known. They are things *had* before they are things cognized" (*Experience and Nature*, p. 21).
23. *Ibid.*, p. 7.
24. *Ibid.*, p. 8.
25. *Ibid.*, p. 8.
26. *Ibid.*, p. 11.
27. *Ibid.*, p. 318.

28. *Erfahrung und Urteil,* ed. L. Landgrebe, Prague: Academia Verlag, 1939.
29. Marvin Farber, *Phenomenology and Existence,* Harper and Row, New York, 1967, p. 131.
30. *Op. cit.,* p. 118.
31. *Art as Experience,* pp. 43-4.
32. *Reconstruction in Philosophy,* p. 86.
33. Cf. John Dewey, *Logic: The Theory of Inquiry,* New York: Henry Holt and Co., 1939, pp. 66-67, 106.
34. John Dewey, *Philosophy and Civilization,* New York: Minton, Balch and Co., 1931, p. 97.
35. Dewey has developed this notion of *pervasive quality* in an extremely provocative essay entitled "Qualitative Thought" which was published in his book, *Philosophy and Civilization,* 1931. In the elaboration of this concept he was heavily indebted to and influenced by W. James who had suggested the germ of the idea in his famous essay "The Place of Affectional Facts in a World of Pure Experience," *Essays in Radical Empiricism,* p. 139.
36. John Dewey, *The Quest for Certainty,* New York: Minton, Balch and Co., 1929, p. 239.

CHAPTER VI

1. *The Quest for Certainty,* Capricorn Books Edition, New York, 1960, p. 295.
2. *Ibid.,* p. 295-6.
3. *Ibid.,* p. 296.
4. *Ibid.,* p. 296.
5. *Experience and Nature,* Dover Publications, New York, 1958, p. 158.
6. *Ibid.,* p. 160.
7. *Ibid.,* p. 421.
8. *Logic.,* p. 104-5.
9. *Ibid.,* p. 107.
10. *Ibid.,* pp. 60-61.
11. *Philosophy and Civilization,* p. 101.
12. *Ibid.,* p. 98.
13. *Ibid.,* p. 98.
14. *Ibid.,* p. 107.
15. *Ibid.,* p. 99.
16. *Ibid.,* p. 99.
17. *Ibid.,* p. 101.
18. *Ibid.,* p. 101.
19. *Ibid.,* p. 105.
20. *Ibid.,* p. 105.
21. *Ibid.,* p. 106-7.
22. *Logic,* pp. 128, 134-35, 189.
23. *Experience and Nature,* p. 151.
24. "Experience, Knowledge and Value: A Rejoinder," *The Philosophy of John Dewey,* ed. Paul Schilpp, pp. 563-4.
25. *Ibid.,* p. 564.
26. *Ibid.,* p. 572.
27. *Ibid.,* footnote, p. 533.

28. *Ibid.*, p. 536.
29. *Ibid.*, p. 537.
30. *Ibid.*, p. 546.
31. *Ibid.*, p. 533.
32. *Ibid.*, p. 548.
33. Dewey had repeatedly to clarify his position on this point in reply to charges from "realists" that for Dewey knowing modifies the object known. On this see: Dewey, "Realism without Monism or Dualism," *Journal of Philosophy*, XIX, June 22, 1922, p. 358, 309. He said in a letter to W. James: "I have repeated ad nauseum that there are existences prior to and subsequent to cognitive states and purposes," Perry, *The Thought and Character of W. James*, II, p. 532.

Dewey insisted that thought reconstructs but never creates. It is the antecedent "subject matter" which undergoes reconstruction and not the object of knowledge. The antecedent subject-matter and the object of knowledge as reconstituted by inquiry are *not* two different things standing one against the other, but the latter is the antecedent subject-matter *as known*—an event with meaning. On this see further:

(i) Dewey, "Some Comments on Philosophical Discussion," *Journal of Philosophy*, XXI, April 10, 1924, pp. 197-209.

(ii) Dewey, "In Reply to Some Criticisms," *Journal of Philosophy*, XXVI, May 8, 1930, p. 273.

(iii) Dewey, "An Empirical Account of Appearance," *Journal of Philosophy*, XXIV, August 18, 1927, p. 458.

34. "Rejoinder," *Schilpp volume*, p. 533.
35. *Ibid.*, p. 534.
36. See Marvin Farber, *Basic Issues of Philosophy*, Harper and Row, New York, 1968, pp. 39-65, 98-120.

CHAPTER VII

1. *The Quest for Certainty*, Minton, Balch and Co., 1929, p. 256.
2. *Ibid.*, p. 252.
3. (i) C. K. Ogden and I. A. Richards, *The Meaning of Meaning*, p. 125.

(ii) A. J. Ayer, *Language, Truth and Logic*, 2nd ed., London, Victor Gollancz, Ltd., 1948, pp. 108-9.

(iii) C. L. Stevenson, *Ethics and Language*, New Haven: Yale University Press, 1944, p. 113.

(iv) C. L. Stevenson, "The Emotive Meaning of Ethical Terms," *Mind*, 1937, pp. 18-19.

(v) C. L. Stevenson, *Facts and Values*, New Haven and London, Yale University Press, 1963, p. 7.

4. *Philosophy and Civilization*, p. 116.
5. A. N. Whitehead, *Science and the Modern World*, The New American Library, New York, 1948, p. 56.
6. *Experience and Nature*, p. 368. Dewey bemoaned this separation of means from ends, instrumentalities from finalities again in his "Reconstruction in Moral Conceptions" in his book *Reconstruction in Philosophy*, Ch. 6, Holt, Rinehart and Winston, Inc., New York, 1920.

7. *Experience and Nature,* p. 369.
8. J. Dewey, "The Construction of Good," *The Quest for Certainty,* Capricorn Books edition, 1960, p. 279.
9. *Ibid.,* p. 282.
10. *Ibid.,* p. 282-3.
11. *Experience and Nature,* p. 366.
12. *Ibid.,* p. 369-70.
13. See R. B. Perry, *General Theory of Value,* New York: Longmans, Green, and Co., 1926, and *Realms of Value,* Cambridge: Harvard University Press, 1954.
14. John Dewey, "The Field of Value," *Value: A Cooperative Inquiry,* ed. Lepley, New York: Columbia University Press, 1949.
15. John Dewey, "Valuation Judgments and Immediate Quality," *Problems of Men,* New York: Philosophical Library, 1949, pp. 250-60.
16. Marvin Farber, *Basic Issues of Philosophy,* Harper and Row, New York, 1968, p. 259.
17. J. Dewey, "The Construction of Good," *The Quest for Certainty,* Capricorn Books, New York, 1960, p. 265.
18. J. Dewey, *Theory of Valuation,* International Encyclopedia of Unified Science, vol. II, no. 4, University of Chicago Press, 1939, p. 58. It is of historical interest to recall that Dewey at first refused to contribute this monograph to the *Encyclopedia of Unified Science* when both E. Nagel and the logical positivist Otto Neurath approached him to do so, on the ground that the logical positivists believed in atomic facts or atomic propositions which, Dewey thought, were non-existent. Only when Neurath solemnly declared, "I *swear* we do not believe in atomic propositions" that Dewey consented to write this monograph and said, "Well, we ought to celebrate," and mixed a strong drink, and made Neurath, who was an abstainer, to take the drink. The whole incident is reported, not without its humor, by E. Nagel in *Dialogue on John Dewey,* ed. Corliss Lamont, Horizon Press, New York, 1959, pp. 11-13.

    Also: cf. John Dewey, "Logical Conditions of a Scientific Treatment of Morality," *Problems of Men,* Philosophical Library, New York, 1946, pp. 211-49.
19. *Experience and Nature,* p. 412.
20. "Rejoinder," *Schilpp volume,* p. 594.

CHAPTER VIII

1. On this, see my paper on "A Note on the Concept of 'Consummatory Experience' in Dewey's Aesthetics," *The Journal of Philosophy,* vol. LXIII, no. 9, April 28, 1966, pp. 225-231.
2. J. Dewey, *Art as Experience,* New York: Minton, Balch and Co., 1934, p. 6.
   * From now on to the end of the chapter, the material has been published in *The Journal of Philosophy,* vol. LXIII, no. 9, April 28, 1966, pp. 226-231. I am indebted to the publisher of *The Journal of Philosophy* for permission to reprint it here.
3. "A Comment on Croce's and Dewey's Aesthetics," *The Journal of Aesthetics & Art Criticism,* 8, 2 (December 1949): 125-129.

4. "Aesthetic Experience as a Primary Phase and as an Artistic Development," *The Journal of Aesthetics & Art Criticism,* 9, 1 (September 1950), 56.
5. *Art as Experience* (New York: Minton, Balch, 1934), p. 17.
6. See Max Black, ed., *Philosophy in America* (Ithaca, N. Y.: Cornell, 1965), pp. 115-133.
7. *Art as Experience,* p. 365. See also *Experience and Nature* (2nd ed., La Salle, Ill.: Open Court, 1958), pp. 354-393.
8. See Christian Zervos, "Conversation with Picasso," in Brewster Ghiselin, ed., *The Creative Process* (New York: The New American Library, 1955), pp. 55-60, esp. 56-57.
9. *Ibid.,* pp. 147-156; from *The Novels & Tales of Henry James,* X (New York: Scribners, 1908).

CHAPTER IX

1. Cf. Marvin Farber, *Naturalism and Subjectivism,* Albany, State University of New York Press, 1968, p. 24-31, *passim.*
2. See *The Aims of Phenomenology,* 1966; *Phenomenology and Existence,* 1967; and *Basic Issues of Philosophy,* 1968.
3. See "Toward a Naturalistic Philosophy of Experience," *Diogenes,* No. 60, Paris, 1967, p. 103-129.
4. B. E. Bykovsky, "The Deobjectification of Philosophy," *Voprosy Filosofii,* 1956, no. 2, p. 142-151, quoted from M. Farber, *Naturalism and Subjectivism,* p. 381.
5. See *Naturalism and Subjectivism,* p. 297-377.
6. *Naturalism and Subjectivism,* p. 386.
7. *Op. cit.,* p. 386.
8. For Farber's appreciative comments on the last part of the trilogy see Marvin Farber, *The Aims of Phenomenology,* Harper and Row, New York, 1966, pp. 229-232.
9. *Naturalism and Subjectivism,* p. 37.
10. *Op. cit.,* p. 51-52.
11. *Basic Issues of Philosophy,* Harper and Row, New York, 1968, p. 212.
12. *Op. cit.,* p. 232.
13. Marvin Farber, "Toward a Naturalistic Philosophy of Experience," *Diogenes,* no. 60, Winter 1967, p. 116.
14. Cf. *Naturalism and Subjectivism,* pp. 92-93.
15. *Op. cit.,* p. 168.
16. *Op. cit.,* p. 159-160.
17. "Toward a Naturalistic Philosophy of Experience," *Op. cit.,* p. 119.
18. For a comprehensive exposition of Farber's philosophical position see (i) *Naturalism and Subjectivism,* pp. 377-386; (ii) *Basic Issues of Philosophy,* p. 184-235. (iii) "Toward a Naturalistic Philosophy of Experience," *Op. cit.,* pp. 126-129. (iv) *Phenomenology and Existence,* pp. 38-112.
19. *Basic Issues of Philosophy,* p. 232.
20. "Toward a Naturalistic Philosophy of Experience," *Op. cit.,* p. 122.
21. *Naturalism and Subjectivism,* pp. 384-5.
22. *Naturalism and Subjectivism,* p. 384.
22(a). "Toward a Naturalistic Philosophy of Experience," *Op. cit.,* p. 126.

22(b). *Naturalism and Subjectivism,* p. 385.

23. *Basic Issues of Philosophy,* p. 230.

CHAPTER X
EPILOGUE

(a) This search for an *absolute beginning* was deliberate and articulate in the case of Husserl but was only implicit in the case of James and Dewey.

1. *Naturalism and Subjectivism,* p. 161.

2. As a valiant champion of the "open-ended" and "ever-not-quite" type of philosophy, James, it may be recalled, had left a note before his death reading:

"There is no conclusion. . . . There are no fortunes to be told, and there is no advice to be given, Farewell."—W. J., "A Pluralistic Mystic." Quoted from Gay Wilson, *William James,* The Viking Press, New York, 1967, p. 495.

3. Cf. James' essay "Ladd's Psychology: Descriptive and Explanatory," *Collected Essays and Reviews,* pp. 344-45.

4. R. B. Perry, *The Thought and Character of William James,* vol. II, Little, Brown, and Co., Boston, 1935, p. 11.

5. *Op. cit.,* p. 541.

INDEX

A

Absolute idealism, 7, 32, 44
Absolute spirit, 54
Advaita vedanta, 54
Aesthetic experience, 103, 105-111 *passim*
Angst (Heidegger), 117

B

Becker, Osker, 125
Bergson, Henri, 17, 60, 61
  his influence on Dewey, 86
Berkeley, George, 38
Black, Max, 152n
Bracketing, phenomenological, 5, 7, 11, 20, 34, 70, 76, 119
Bradley, F. H., 32
Brentano, Franz, 12, 57
Broad, C. D., 91
Bykovsky, B. E., 116

C

Categorial intuition (Husserl), 39
Cohen, Marshall, 107, 109
Consciousness, 8, 12, 20
  James' analysis, 14, 15, 29, 30, 35, 37
Constitution (Husserl), 12, 34, 43, 75, 119, 131
Consummatory experience, Dewey's concept of, 103, 104, 106, 107, 109, 111
Contextualism (Dewey), 82, 85

D

Descriptive phenomenology, 5, 6, 33
  psychology, 5, 33
Descartes, René, 7, 18, 32, 49, 93, 118

Dewey, John, 44, 130, 134, 135, 118
  on aesthetic experience, 103, 105-111
  on immediate experience, 12, 18, 67-79, 92-94
  on inquiry, 80-92
  on knowledge, 32, 39, 80-92
  on truth, 44, 90, 91
  on value-experience, 95-102
Dualism, 38

E

Edie, James M., 141n
Ego, 57, 58
  Husserl's pure Ego, 20
  Husserl's three egos, 19
  James' analysis, 27, 29, 30
  James' critique of Kant's doctrine, 22, 23
  Transcendental, 8, 14, 34, 36, 76
Eidetic reduction, 7, 11, 119
Empiricism, 32, 49
Emotivism, 96
Entfremdung (Heidegger), 117
Entschlossenheit (Heidegger), 117
Epoché (Husserl), 63, 70, 96, 119, 121, 131, 141n
Essence (Husserl), 11, 12
Experience, Dewey's analysis of, 12, 18, 67-79, 92-94, 95-102, 103, 105-111
  Farber on, 10-11
  Humean conception of, 6
  Husserl's theory of, 6-9 *passim*, 11
  James' analysis, 9, 10, 13-17, 30, 34, 36, 40
  Of the Self (James), 19-23

F

Farber, Marvin, on experience, 10-11
  on fallacy of 'illicit ignorance,' 9, 71

R

Radical empiricism (James), 21, 25, 30-31, 50-51, 61, 133
Rationalism, 32, 49, 50
Rational intuition, 11
Rationality, James' analysis, 50, 53, 54-56, 60, 133
Realism, 81-83
Reality, James' analysis, 7, 49-53, 56-60, 133
Reduction, eidetic, 7, 11, 119
mechanical, 38
phenomenological, 6, 20, 119, 120, 132
transcendental, 11, 120
Reichenbach, Hans, 91
Romain, Jules, 109
Romanell, Patrick, 106
Royce, Josiah, 32
Russell, Bertrand, 80, 90-91
Ryle, Gilbert, 18; on self, 19

S

Santayana, George, 16, 78; on Dewey's naturalism, 71, 73
Sartre, Jean-Paul, 18, 117, 125
Scheler, Max, 117
Schiller, F. C. S., 44
Schuld (Heidegger), 117
Schutz, Alfred, 141n
Sein-zum-Tode (Heidegger), 117

Self, problem of, 18-19; James' analysis, 21-22, 24-31, 37
Self-givenness (Husserl), 34
Sorge (Heidegger), 117
Spencer, Herbert, 50, 52
Spinoza, Benedict (Baruch), 54
Supernaturalism, James on, 61-62
Synthetic Unity of Apperception (Kant), 13

T

Transcendental constitution (Husserl), 11
idealism (Husserl), 6, 7, 32
phenomenology (Husserl), 35
subjectivity (Husserl), 43
Truth, 44-48, 90

V

Value-experience, Dewey's analysis, 95-102

W

Whitehead, Alfred North, 135
Wild, John, 141n
Wilshire, Bruce, 141n
Wittgenstein, Ludwig, 18, 21; on the self, 19

Z

Zervos, Christian, 152n